LITTLE JIMMY

MAY, BURBANK AND BOONE

Remembrances

To Bev,

A fellow member of the Smoker's 50-50 Club.

J.E. Martinelli

LITTLE ITALY

MAY, BURBANK AND BOONE

Remembrances

JOE MARTINELLI

Rockhouse Press

ISBN: 1-59268-042-9

Rockhouse Press
New York, New York

GMAPublishing.com
Check out our website
GMA is a global publishing company
Our books are available and distributed around the world and can
be found on the internet at Amazon, Barnes and Noble and any
major bookseller.

GMAPublishing@aol.com

Cover Layout: Cecilia Brendel
Back Cover street sign and flag design: Jamie Poole
Front Cover street scene design: Joe Martinelli
Manuscript Assistant: John Beanblossom

Printed in the United States of America

This book is dedicated to my parents
Stella and Nick Martinelli

Special thanks to my wife Barbara and my teacher and friend
Lisa Chewning for their support during this long process.

However, this book would never have happened without the
historical interest of Professor Emeritus Zane Miller, at the
University of Cincinnati and an article in the
Cincinnati Enquirer.

Thank you Jim Knippenberg!

Author's Note:

Haven't you looked back on your life and said, "Those were my finest years"? For me, my finest years were my formative years in grade and high school. The fact that I lived most of those years in Little Italy, a community within the predominantly German city of Cincinnati, Ohio, makes it more interesting and unique to me.

We lived in a ghetto but didn't realize it. Our Italian parents probably experienced some discrimination and prejudice, but we children were oblivious to it; we were in our own world. I recently took a look back at that, MY WORLD, and felt such a surge of passion that I knew I had to share it with others.

My world was:

LITTLE ITALY – MAY, BURBANK AND BOONE

PRELUDE:

Going Home Again

Like most people, my childhood contains its share of good and bad happenings. However, as I grow older and mellower, I tend to recall mainly the joys of my youth. I particularly remember the fascinating individuals who shared their time with me. These people and our experiences together helped shape my character. Does that mean, therefore, that they share some responsibility for my successes and failures in life? Well, maybe the few successes, but I take full responsibility for my failures. Oh yes, I've had a full platter of those. So I thought that one way of repaying these wonderful people for the privilege of knowing them would be for me to introduce them to you. That was my logic in writing these stories and, after reading them, I hope that you agree.

These are recollections of incidents and characters; relatives, friends, teachers and neighbors that I knew while growing up in Cincinnati, Ohio. My "Little Italy" was in the eastern suburb of Walnut Hills. Not to be confused with the other Little Italy on Queen City Avenue in the western part of town. There were two Little Italy's in Cincinnati in those days.

The time frame for my stories is during and after the Great Depression and World War II. Besides those great epochs, it was unique because my story also preceded television. *Radio* was our king. Street cars, trains and buses were the standard means of travel. And, as for the political slogan, "A car in every garage," hell, who could afford a car? Or, for that matter, who had a garage? There were very few cars in Little Italy.

Naturally, it was a slower lifestyle than today's, but we didn't know that at the time. Those of us who listened to *Buck Rogers* on the radio may have dreamed or hoped that life would "speed up" in the future. Other than that, we didn't pay much attention to *time*. We were only concerned about *now*. After sports, music and girls, the possibility and then the reality of War got very little of *our* attention. Oh, we heard about Hitler, Tojo and Mussolini, and even kept up with the latest Battle News. But, as I said and, as you will discover for yourselves, *we* had other things on our minds at the time.

The Author

CHAPTER 1

My Home Town

ARGUMENTS? OH YES, ALWAYS. FIGHTS? Never, because that wasn't our style. My buddies and I prided ourselves in being "lovers, not fighters." Yet the tough guys in our neighborhood, and we had them, never picked on us. Why? Because we all lived in "Little Italy." And we were respected for that. We had the same rights and privileges, though unwritten and unspoken, as anyone else who lived there. It made no difference whether you were Italian, Irish, German or Negro. If you lived in Little Italy, you were "family."

Little Italy, in the 1940's, covered an area of approximately three square miles. Basically residential, it consisted of two and three storied family houses, a few unattached garages, several large apartment buildings, a church, six grocery stores, several light industries, including a printing company, two bakeries and a half dozen other small businesses. All were spread over a north to south and east to west grid of streets and alleys. Two landmarks dominated the area: the five storied Mayburn Apartment Building and, directly across the street, Our Lady of Mt. Carmel Catholic

Church. Both buildings were located on opposite corners of May and Burbank Streets.

Some Cincinnatians didn't see Little Italy the same way that I did. They were more familiar with its reputation for saloons, beer gardens and nightclubs. Situated on the corner of Boone and Burbank Streets, in the heart of Little Italy, was one of the best nightspots in town, Spider's Cafe. Spider's, as it was called, had a reputation for good times that began during Prohibition and continued into the 1930's and 40's. Over those years Spider's did make the transition from booze and "hot" stage shows and dancing to a lunch and dinner restaurant featuring good steaks at a reasonable price. My mom favored Belle's, Spider's sister-in-law and cook, roast beef sandwiches, especially when Mom was pregnant with the twins.

Conveniently, party goers leaving Spider's could go across to the opposite corner of Boone and Burbank Streets, and continue their play at Jiddy's Bar and Garden. When they wanted to move on, only a half block farther up the hill was Big Mike's Saloon. On the corner of May and Burbank Streets was another watering hole, Delcarpen's Bar. Across the street from "Dell's," on the other corner of May and Burbank, was Our Lady Of Mt. Carmel Catholic Church. Behind the Church, across the alley and extending all the way to the very top of Burbank Street Hill, was yet another favorite drinking place, One Arm Tony's beer garden.

In case you lost count that was five saloons and bars within one block of the church. And I didn't include my Grandpa's favorite hangout, Louie's Pool Room. Louie's was next door to Spider's on Boone Street and where, if one still had a thirst after the bars had closed, and Louie knew you, a glass of homemade (Dego Red) wine might be available. My Grandpa counted on it! All these establishments, Spider's, Jiddy's, Big Mike's, Dell's, One Arm Tony's and Louie's co-existed with the church, on just three city streets, May, Burbank and Boone.

Of course, these establishments were also our adult neighborhood hangouts. Our grandfathers, fathers, uncles, cousins and older brothers would go for a glass of beer or wine and socialize after work or dinner, every day or night. You can see why some outsiders would believe Little Italy was a fun place to go, but to others, I would learn later, it was a place to fear and avoid. There were stories of drunken fights and the like, even some shootings during the Prohibition that gave Little Italy a shady reputation. But for me it was the most wonderful and exciting place in the whole world.

CHAPTER 2

My Family - La Familia

LITTLE ITALY, WITH ITS WEB of intersecting streets and alleys, was home to mostly Italian families and, as I said, with a few German, Irish and Negro families sprinkled in. Several of these non-Italians played major roles in my life and I will introduce them to you later. Since I spent the first thirteen years of my life in Little Italy, its unique environment, my acquaintances and experiences, certainly provided the foundation for my character.

Of course, we all want to believe that we have evolved into someone better than we might have under different circumstances. But are any of us really in a position to know for sure if we have succeeded or not? Can we really be objective about ourselves? It would be damn presumptuous of me to think that the good always out-weighed the bad in my life. In fact, that would be an outright lie. No confessions here; just read on and you be the judge.

My father, who I lovingly remember as Poppa Nick, came to this country from Bari, Italy, in 1921. A product of a large (seven brothers and one sister) Catholic and struggling family. What other kind was there back in the Old Country in those days?

He had been an Italian soldier from the state of Puglio and he fought against the Austrians for three years in World War I. Poppa Nick was on the front lines for three of those four years. Lucky for me he survived to join his six older brothers in America, in the beautiful and peaceful city of Cincinnati, Ohio.

My mother, Stella, was a first generation Italian-American with a particle of Slovenian (or Austrian?) thrown in from my Grandma Anna's side of the family. Just enough Germanic or Slavic blood to provide Grandma, Mom and me, with our deep blue eyes. That was a strange combination in Little Italy in those days. I always believed it gave me a slight edge over my brown-eyed Italian buddies. "Where did you get those big blue bedroom eyes?" some ladies were soon to ask. Maybe too soon, I might add.

The fact that I was the eldest child and a boy at that, assured me of princely treatment by my family, especially by Poppa Nick. That's the Italian way, the son is his pride, if not always his joy. My sister Anita (Ninny), was four years younger than me, and the twins Marie (Ree Ree), and Marguerite (Margy), were ten years younger than me. Mom and Pop had their hands full, but they would tell you they loved every minute of it. Do all parents believe that? Yes, I guess we do.

Poppa Nick's barber shop was the fulfillment of his trench-war dreams. Of course, he expected me to be a barber and to follow in his footsteps. You know what I mean, the old saying, "If you don't have a trade, you'll starve to death." And so I was a barber for a while. But as others have found in their own lives, Pop's dream was not my dream. And when I eventually left his barber shop for a job with a large corporation, I think I broke his heart. And he never gave up trying to lure me back to his shop. He couldn't understand why I would want to work for someone else. Why did I?

I know I wanted security, paid vacations and those other magical things called "benefits." A barber in those days worked ten hours a day, six days a week and received none of the above. Only my engagement and impending marriage finally alerted Poppa Nick that I was going to leave the shop. Shouldn't he have expected something like this? After all, didn't he do the same thing himself when he left his mother and a sweetheart in Italy in 1921 to come to America? He finally gave me his blessing and approved of my going to work for General Electric in Evendale,

Ohio, where they manufactured jet engines. Did he see a little of himself in me at that time? I believe so.

My family always came first with me, but not like it did for my father. I wouldn't kiss anyone's ass, not even a relative's, but I thought Poppa Nick did. Maybe I was blinded by a cultural or generation gap, but I never could understand his kowtowing to his older brothers and their children. I guess he was guided by the Old Country ways, you know the Italian "Familia" thing. For example, on a Sunday, his only day off, he would pack his tools in a paper bag and go to his brother Louie's house downtown in the West End to cut everybody's hair, his brother's, his nephews and his nieces, for free. He would take me with him on these excursions, of course. My aunt Elizabeth made the best ravioli in the whole world and anything she cooked was always a treat. Visiting the West End was how I learned to "Watch your car for a dime, Mister?" when the Cincinnati Reds played a home baseball game at Crosley Field. Yes, my cousins Tony and Joe taught me a lot of fun things. But still I was never like Poppa Nick in his giving way. Perhaps that was my loss, who knows?

When his nephew Marco was on leave from the mental hospital and needed a place to stay, Pop took him in. When his sister-in-law Mary needed somewhere to stay before she went to

California, Pop took her in, and the list goes on and on. During World II, when you couldn't mail packages directly to Italy, my Pop would faithfully send money and candy to his brother's family in Bari, Italy, through the Catholic Relief Agency (I'm talking five or ten dollars here, not thousands) via Brazil or Argentina. Do you have the picture of this man yet? If not, I believe it will get clearer as we go on.

The women in my family, my momma Stella, and my younger sisters Anita, Marie and Marguerite were my "special loves" and I will nurture that joy forever. Anita usually managed to bring her girlfriends into the house when my buddies and I were there. We called them "punks" because they were two or three years younger than us. Truthfully, at the time, I generally thought they were a pain in the ass. That said, I must be honest and tell you that two of my buddies were soon to think differently. Tony Wass ended up going with Cheri the "Fawn" and Tony D'Ang dated and eventually married Millie the "Redhead."

At that time, I wasn't too fond of redheads. Boy, how that was to change. I was somewhat put off by their opaque and fair white skin and freckles. And it certainly would piss us off when Tony D'Ang wouldn't go swimming with the rest of us because "Millie can't swim in the direct sun." "Who gives a shit," we would say. Well, apparently he did. And sure enough, Tony and Millie would show up at Phillip's Pool or at Coney Island in the late afternoon or early evening. I never thought about this at the time, but what did they do all day before coming to the pool? Why, of course, they probably went to a movie, a matinee.

I would tease Momma that she must have been part Gypsy because we were always moving from one place to another. I don't think she appreciated my comments at all. What made me say that to her? Well, Mom and Pop lived in two different houses on Boone Street, two different apartments and on two different floors in the Mayburn Apartment Building on Burbank, in a house down at the south end of May Street and finally in a house up on Kenton Street. All the above in Little Italy.

And that's not counting when they were just married and lived in Avondale, or when the twins arrived and we moved to the Projects, in English Woods, for about a year before returning to Little Italy. I guess the real reason for all these moves was that Momma and Poppa were raising an ever-growing family. They did the best they could, with not enough money coming in and with landlords that didn't want children living on their properties.

I remember Poppa telling a customer at the barber shop that years ago his brother-in-law, my Uncle Julius, said that there was a house for rent on the other side of McMillan Street, not in Little Italy. Both Poppa and Uncle Julius went up to see the house after dinner that same evening. The landlady was very cordial, showed them the apartment and told my Poppa what she expected in rent. Both Uncle Julius and Poppa were very pleased because the apartment was large enough for all of us and the price was right. But when Poppa mentioned that his "wife and children would be very happy here," she replied, "Oh, I'm sorry, but I don't rent to people with children."

After he got over the initial shock of her statement, my Poppa responded, "Please don't rent it out to someone else for an hour and I'll go home and kill the sons of bitches and be right back." I would have loved to have seen the expression on her face. That folks was an example of Poppa Nick's "Depression humor."

CHAPTER 3

Grandma Anna

LIVING IN THE MAYBURN APARTMENTS had its advantages, the greatest of which was that my Grandma Anna and Grandpa Tony were the resident janitors. This meant to me that I owned the place. Considering how curious I was at four to nine years of age when we lived there, for me, it was a giant Toyland. Mom, Pop, my sister Anita and I lived in two different apartments and on two different floors over a span of five years.

After Mom would feed me breakfast, I would dash downstairs to Grandma's basement apartment. Invariably, she would ask, "Jo Jo, have you eaten?" And my answer was always "No, Grandma, can I eat with you?" She would smile the smile of loving grandmothers everywhere and set another plate, bowl or cup for her grandson. She loved the company of her grandson and the many questions he would ask. We talked about everything.

I need to explain why she would set a cup for me and not a glass. I did not then, nor do I now, like to drink milk. The only way my mother was able to get me to drink milk as a child was to mix it with coffee and sugar. Supposedly some Mediterranean people have difficulty digesting cow's milk and I was one of them.

Grandma Anna was my best friend in the whole world. And her building, The Mayburn, was my castle. We lived in a two room apartment and shared a bath with the neighboring two room apartment. For several years, we lived on the third floor and later moved to the fifth floor. And regardless of when I would go up or down the steps, it seemed that Grandma Anna would be sweeping or scrubbing the steps on one floor or another. Oh, how I wish I could hear her say to me once again, "Don't step where it's wet, Jo Jo."

The main entrance of the Mayburn Apartments was on the Burbank Street side of the building. Burbank is a pretty steep hill starting at the top at One Arm Tony's on Kenton Street all the way down past May Street, the church and the Mayburn, and down again to Spider's Cafe and Jiddy's at the bottom of the hill at Boone Street.

Grandma and Grandpa's apartment had a separate entrance on Burbank nearer to the alley. You actually had to step down three steps to enter at that point because the apartment wasn't at ground level until you reached the alley behind Spider's.

After reaching Boone Street, Burbank became a viaduct over the Merkle Brother's Pipe Foundry, the Ditto Press Company and the main railroads from downtown Cincinnati to the Northeast. On the west side of the viaduct, Burbank Street ended with its intersection with Symmes Street. On the west side of Symmes was Little Italy's very own version of the Rock of Gibraltar. We called it "Goose Neck Hill." To a seven year old like me, Goose Neck Hill looked to be hundreds of feet high and easily the home of some prehistoric monsters or even King Kong himself.

On the other side of Symmes, Burbank actually narrows to alley size and meanders along the southern side of Goose Neck Hill and makes its way to the southwest side of the hill. That was where the big Davis Brothers Tailoring Company was located. Poppa had worked there as a presser at one time and Uncle Julius, a master tailor, worked there for many years as did many other men and women from our neighborhood. Others worked under the Burbank Viaduct at the Merkle Brothers Pipe Foundry or at the Ditto Press Company. Do you remember ditto and carbon copies? My cousin Helen worked as a secretary at Ditto Press for many years. It seems so strange to me today that so many people worked within walking distance from their homes. How times and habits have changed.

Burbank Street continued eastward from the top of the hill at Kenton Street, across the street from One Arm Tony's, for another block and downhill toward Florence and Gilbert Avenues. That was the route we took each day walking to and from home to Windsor Grade School.

Momma and Poppa said that I spoke and understood Italian fairly well before I started going to school. Grandma Anna and I would converse in Italian and she taught me to pray in Italian. However, once I started going to school, my ability to converse in Italian disappeared. I wonder why that happened? Was it because I was so proud of learning to speak English better than Poppa? Or was it because I was embarrassed about my Italian background and language and purposely allowed it to slip away from me? An interesting psychological question, don't you think? I'll have to ask a shrink about that someday.

Grandma Anna bore sixteen children in her lifetime, including (I believe) a set of twins. Only four of her children survived beyond the age of twenty: Uncle John, Aunt Mary, Momma and the baby, my Uncle Albert. Some died as a result of the great flu epidemic of 1918 in New York and others died as a result of poor living conditions (bad water, disease, etc.) in the coal mining territory of Kentucky.

Grandma was born near the city of Trieste, in what is now part of Italy, but was then part of Slovenia, a state in the Austrian-Hungarian Empire. She was half Italian and half Slovenian, I think. To this day, my Momma, Aunt Mary and Uncle Albert can't agree whether Grandma was half Slovenian, Croatian, Austrian or all of the above. I thought you deserved to know that.

Two of Grandma's husbands had come from Venice. Her first husband, a sailor, had drowned at sea. Anna wrote her husband's friend Tony in the United States and told him of his death. Tony, an ex-sailor, wrote back and said, "Come to America with the children and we will get married." She did and they did. Do people still do things like that anymore?

In Lynch Mines, only a mining camp at the time but now the city of Lynch, Kentucky, Grandpa Tony worked in the mines and Grandma took in boarders in their Company owned house. She said that cooking for the miners, whether German, Russian, Polish or Italian helped her to become a good cook of soups and stews. I can tell you firsthand that her cooking was wonderful, especially with a fresh loaf of Italian bread from Stephen's Bakery. My oh my, I can almost smell those exotic aromas still. Grandma also spoke all those languages fluently.

Grandma was a lot of things, as you have or will yet discover, but it always amazed me that she would also pray from missals in all those languages each day of her life. I never understood why she did it. Why not just her Italian Missal? I wish now that I had asked her. That was some mystery and she was some woman.

Grandma Anna was a big woman physically and Grandpa Tony was just the opposite. He was small in stature yet very strong for his size. I guess his strength came from mining all those years. But still, his friends in Louie's Pool Room called him Shorty when they wanted to tease him. However, no one but her closest friends would dare call my Grandma anything but Anna or Mrs. Vianello. Why? Because she was as strong as most men and her tongue was as sharp as a knife. She was friendly to all she met, but don't cross her nor let her hear that you wronged her husband, her children or her grandchildren.

A classic example of my Grandma Anna in action was the time when we lived on Kenton Street and she dropped by the house to see us. Momma happened to mention that the expensive meat that she had purchased at the German butcher shop on McMillan Street had been "tough as shoe leather." Without a word to

Momma when Grandma left the house, she headed straight for the butcher shop.

We learned later that Grandma told the butcher who she was and then said, and I quote, "Gott dammit, you son of a bitch, Honey, don't you ever sell my daughter tough meat again!" That folks was my Grandma Anna, God Bless her. She was a screen of protection for her family like no one I have ever known. Were other Grandmothers like that? Are all grandparents like that? Am I like that? I don't think so.

CHAPTER 4

Momma Stella - A Dapper Flapper

GROWING UP IN COAL MINING COUNTRY in the early 1900's was damn hard for most everyone. Mom and her one year older sister, my Aunt Mary, would carry water for a mile from the springs or creeks several times a day for Grandma Anna, her family and her boarders. They went to whatever schools might be available to them but certainly no further than the fourth grade. At that time there wasn't a hell of a lot of educational services to be had in that part of the world. Theirs was the proverbial school of hard knocks and they learned very quickly that hard work was to be their normal way of life.

Somehow Grandpa Tony was able to find work in Cincinnati. Stella and Mary found work at a laundry on Symmes Street. Later they became telephone operators for the Cincinnati Bell Telephone Company and worked together at the Walnut Hills Exchange. Uncle Johnny, the oldest, got a job as a truck driver and Uncle Albert, the youngest, went to Windsor Grade School. Living became a lot easier for everyone.

For one thing Momma and Aunt Mary started to go out on dates. Aunt Mary's boyfriend, my Uncle Julius Lombardi, arranged a blind date for Momma. About that, Momma once said, "I will never forget that day when we lived on Boone Street; the door opened and in walked the most handsome man I had ever seen." That man was Nicolo Martinelli, who became the love of her life and my Poppa Nick.

Unlike Grandma Anna, my mother Stella was very shy. So when fate presented this mature, newly arrived from Italy, good looking man on her doorstep, she knew he was the only man for her. Stella was eighteen and Nicolo was twenty-nine. They had only dated for two months when he asked Stella to marry him. When she agreed, he borrowed a few dollars from his buddy and nephew Joe, and they were married across the river in Covington, Kentucky. Joe and his girlfriend (later his wife) Mildred were their witnesses. The year was 1928. I came along a year later, as did "The Great Crash."

CHAPTER 5

Nick The Barber

POPPA NICK'S BARBER SHOP WAS part of the Kemper Lane Hotel and fronted on East McMillan Street, the main drag of the Peebles Corner business district. His customers were drawn from all over Walnut Hills but especially the two major hotels, the Kemper Lane Hotel and two blocks farther down McMillan Street, the Alms Hotel. There was also the residential Harrison Club for single men only, and the Power's Acting Studio, run by Tyrone Power's parents, around the corner on Kemper Lane. The Kemper Lane Hotel's restaurant and bar, called The Spa, also provided walk-in customers and had its own access door to the barber shop. Henry Schnikner worked the barber shop's second chair. The third chair was used by a variety of barbers over the years, but Poppa Nick had "Father & Son" plans for his shop, and I was the Son part of those plans and for that chair.

Poppa Nick held several jobs after he came from Italy in 1921. He had worked for the railroad for awhile but didn't like the hard physical labor it entailed. After that a friend got him a job working for the Davis Tailoring Company. Nick was still pressing clothes at Davis Tailoring when his older brother Sebastian, who had his own barber shop in Avondale, encouraged him to go to barber college to learn the trade. Sebastian said he would help finance tuition. Nick saw his opportunity and took it. He graduated, passed his State Board Examination and became a licensed barber.

Nick's first job as a barber was downtown on Broadway and Fourth Street. It was at that time that he met the young girl Stella, fell in love and got married. After that he went to work for Mr. Bellchore on McMillan Street between May and Kenton Streets. It was there that Nick started giving the stylish lady's cut of the 20's and 30's called "the Bob." He soon became very popular with the ladies in the neighborhood. Sometimes there were as many women as there were men waiting for haircuts at Mr. Bellchore's Barber Shop.

I don't believe having women around the barber shop was appreciated by the much older Mr. Bellchore. In fairness to Mr. Bellchore, that probably also reflected the feelings of the men from Little Italy, where his clientele mostly came from.

So, tall, dark and handsome Nick moved on. This time Nick went to work at Steve Ballanti's barber shop on Gilbert Avenue near Peebles Corner. My sister Anita and I remember

Steve very well. Occasionally, and always on a Thursday, Pop would bring Steve home for a spaghetti dinner. Ah, now I know why he always came on Thursdays! We always had pasta two times a week, Thursdays and Sundays. Steve probably felt Thursday was the most convenient time for all concerned since Sunday was their only day off. It makes sense to me. And yes, Steve was that kind of thoughtful guy.

My sister Anita and I remember how Steve would put coins in our hands when he came into our apartment. They were from his tips at the barber shop. Then Anita and I would make signs to each other under the table to show how much each of us got. He never failed us, did he, Anita? We sure looked forward to having Steve come to our house for dinner. Thank you, Steve, wherever you are.

An amazing and ironic story about Pop and Steve cries out to be told, and so I will. During World War I, they both served their countries in their respective armies. For those of you non-historians, allow me to say, Poppa Nick fought for Italy and Steve fought for Austria. While working for Steve, my Pop mentioned being in the great battle on the Piave River, in the Dolomite Region of the Alps. Steve said he fought there, also. Poppa mentioned a particularly bloody mountain that he fought his way up and back down again, and Steve said he had fought on that same mountain.

Can you imagine how these two men felt knowing they both survived that terrible battle as enemies, and here they were, in yet another country, working together side by side? It would be impossible to second guess what their thoughts were on that strange day, or for that matter, what wondrous discussions they may have had over the span of years that they worked together. One thing for sure, they both knew that they were damn lucky to be alive and working together in America. Ernest Hemingway, who had been in those mountains too, would have had a field day with their stories.

CHAPTER 6

Anita - Younger Sister and Friend

MY SISTER ANITA IS FOUR years younger than me. When we lived in the Mayburn Apartments, she and I shared a day bed in the kitchen. In the morning Momma would fold up the bed and push it against the wall. She had a cloth cover over the bed during the day. Ninny, as I called her because as a kid I couldn't pronounce Anita, was my faithful companion.

Momma would charge me to look out for her welfare. Many a Saturday morning we would walk up to Peebles Corner with enough money to get us into the Eden Theater, probably a dime each, at eleven in the morning when the movies opened. Momma would either pack us a lunch or give us enough money to buy ourselves a hamburger to take in with us or buy a skyscraper ice cream cone on the corner of McMillan and Gilbert Avenue afterwards. We often sat through a double feature of movies (Tom Mix, etc.) and several serials and cartoons. Frankly, the Eden Theater was our baby sitter.

I would take Ninny's hand and walk up May Street to McMillan and on up to Peebles Corner and the Eden Theater.

Sometimes we went with other kids from our neighborhood, taking different routes each time just for the adventure. When we found that we were really early, we would walk slowly past all the stores and shops on McMillan, looking into their windows until we reached the Eden. Other times we would walk up alleys and side-streets to get there. Each time and each route was great fun and very special to us.

There were times when Momma would pay an older girl in our neighborhood to go along and keep an eye on us. We didn't understand why some of the girls were so popular once we got to the movies. We didn't realize at the time that older kids did other things besides watch movies at the Eden, Paramount or Orpheum Movie Theaters. Yes, we had some very popular neighborhood girls.

Ninny and I did the dishes at our house. We were supposed to take turns washing and drying, but I tried my best to get Ninny to do the washing. I hated that. The great thing about doing dishes, for us, was singing. And we did it real good folks. "Pardon me, boy, is that the Chattanooga Choo Choo?" Remember that one?

Momma had a crush on Lanny Ross, the great radio show singer, and his theme song was her favorite, "T'was the Isle of Capri, where I met her." "Neath the shade of an old Apple Tree." We would sing every night and loved every minute of it. When we have reunions now, for whatever purpose, we usually don't part until we sing some of the old dishwashing songs again. Once more, for the good times, Ninny, what do you say?

CHAPTER 7

Castle Mayburn

MY SISTER ANITA TELLS ME that I put a romantic slant on all things seen, heard or experienced pertaining to Little Italy, and maybe she's right. Wait, before you throw this book aside, let me offer an explanation of why this could be so. How many of you grew up in a castle? Well, as a child, I felt like I did. My castle was the Mayburn Apartment Building with its clock tower high above all the other houses and townspeople of Little Italy.

It actually made that kind of impression on me. Take, for example, the top floor where Momma and the other women did their laundry. Momma and the other ladies boiled and scrubbed their clothes and diapers in giant copper tubs. Oh, it got hot and steamy in the laundry room at times, and the smells weren't always pleasant either, but it was still one of my favorite places for adventure.

There were a half dozen small windows overlooking the northern and western parts of my neighborhood. I pretended to defend my castle using all those windows as gun ports. Sometimes

I pretended to be on the top of the Alps where my Poppa fought in the Great War. I would be a machine gunner one minute or I might use my French 75's against the Kaiser's armies. Yet another day I might be defending my castle from the Vikings with English long bows.

Sometimes I pretended to be a sailor at the top of a mast on a fast sailing ship like my Grandpa Tony had sailed on before he came to America. I knew what his ships looked like because Grandpa had been a ship's carpenter before he jumped ship in New York, and he made many models of sailing ships as a hobby. Some of Grandpa's ships were displayed in a bank window in downtown Cincinnati. He even put some ships inside bottles. So, you see, I knew what a main mast was and where a warship's gun ports were and that kind of stuff. I constantly played "what if" games without knowing that I was doing so.

As I had said, we had lived on two different floors at the Mayburn, the third and fifth. Grandma Anna lived in an alley side apartment on the basement level reserved for the janitor of the Mayburn Apartments. My sister Anita remembers the Mayburn as a tenement building, but I don't buy that. When I think of tenement houses or buildings, I think of New York City and its row upon row, block upon block of brick and greystone buildings.

Of course, my sister didn't have the benefit of growing up as a Charles Lindburg pilot one day or a French Foreign Legionnaire the next, or a Kentucky Mountain Man another because, as you see, my sister is a girl. My other sisters, the twins, Marie and Marguerite, hadn't been born yet.

Even after the twins were born when Momma would wash diapers, I would go along and look out the windows high above Burbank. I could see all the way up May Street and see the streetcars on McMillan Street, three blocks way. And when I looked down Burbank, past Boone, I could see the bridge all the way over to Symmes Street and the whole top of Goose Neck Hill.

I don't know what my sister Anita saw or thought when she looked out those windows, surely she had her own fantasies, but I know what I saw and believed. Because of my self-assumed castle duties as pilot, soldier, frontiersman and, oh yes, cowboy and sometimes Indian, one can understand why I might see my life somewhat differently than my sister Anita.

The other truth about how I viewed my childhood is a sociological one. I saw people in "my village" differently than they saw me. They didn't have the advantages I had. They didn't have my view of the world from the laundry room. They also didn't have a Grandpa Tony, a Venetian sailor, who not only had sailed the world but told his grandson great tales of the sea. Like that time he sailed on the Arctic Ocean and it was so cold that his "spit turned to ice before it hit the deck" of his ship, as he told me.

When I was with Grandpa in his workshop in the basement of the Mayburn, I would pretend the basement was my dungeon, and the great big coal bin in the furnace room was a coal mine in Lynch, Kentucky, where he had worked when he first came to this country.

No, my sister and my friends didn't have the opportunity to grow up in the rich and exciting atmosphere that I created for myself in the Mayburn Apartments. So it is only natural that Anita's view of those times would be quite different than mine. I sincerely regret that my sisters didn't have the opportunities that were showered on me as the son and grandson in those days. I must confess that I'll always be grateful that it did happen to me.

CHAPTER 8

My Mayburn Point Of View

I THINK MY MOST FAVORITE adventure of all was just looking out the Mayburn's laundry room windows as far as I could see. Like way up May Street, all the way to McMillan Street and the streetcar lines or down Burbank, over the Viaduct to Symmes Street and the gigantic Gooseneck Hill. Sometimes I would just look straight down as far as I could, considering I wasn't allowed to stick my head out the window.

My fascination with looking straight down was because Mikey lived across Burbank in his grandfather's, Big Mike's building, above Big Mike's Saloon. We were always looking for one another because we played together a lot. I also played in the alley behind our building, but I couldn't look straight down to it. I couldn't look straight down on May Street because that was on the other side of the steps and hallway from the laundry room.

If I could look straight down on May Street, I would be looking for Joe Joe and Andee who lived next door to the Mayburn, up on the second floor. They even had a yard, too. It was a narrow strip that extended from May Street all the way back to the alley. We didn't have any yard at the Mayburn Apartments. Our makeshift playground was the street in front of the grocery store on the ground floor, on the May Street side of the Mayburn Building, and in front of Our Lady of Mt. Carmel Church.

I wasn't allowed to play in the street on wash days because Momma wanted to be able to keep an eye on me and my little sister, Anita. That was OK with me because I could always entertain myself by the windows. My twin baby sisters, Marie and Marguerite, were usually cared for by Ann Behan in front of her steps in the alley behind the Mayburn where she lived or in our apartment.

On days when I could see Mikey on the sidewalk down below on Burbank Street, I would ask, "Momma, can I go out and play?"

"Not now, Jo Jo, maybe later," she would reply.

"But Mikey's standing in front of his grandpa's saloon," I would beg. "Please let me go over and play, I promise to be careful," I would whine.

"No, Jo Jo and don't forget to play with your sister, Anita," she would add.

"Can I just go down to the front door and tell him that I can play with him later? I promise I won't go across the street and I'll come right back," I would pledge. And more times than not, she relented.

"OK, but you come right back up here, do you hear me? And don't you even go down the entrance steps to the sidewalk, do you understand?"

"I won't, I promise," I said and dashed for the hallway.

Down and down the six flights of stairs I would fly until I reached the building entrance door. I would pull it open and hope Mikey was still there. "Mikey," I would yell. He would wave hello.

"Come on over," he usually said.

"I can play later, Momma's washing clothes and I have to watch my sister," I would explain. He understood because this ritual was played out weekly. "OK, I'll probably be in the back yard," he would remark as he walked back into his grandpa's saloon.

Now, Mikey's back yard was really a concrete courtyard between his grandpa's house above the saloon and his two rental houses next door. The back doors of the rental houses opened up on the same courtyard. Naturally, all of that encompassed what Mikey and I considered our playground. And when it rained, we had the long hallway leading from the courtyard to May Street where we played. This hallway was the entrance to another rental apartment above the saloon and next to Big Mike's son's business, Anthony's Dry Cleaners that was situated on the corner of May and Burbank Streets. And that hallway apartment was where Annie, the girl in blue lived.

Annie was the inspiration for a song titled "The Girl In Blue" that Mikey and I wrote. When and how this inspiration came about I am almost ashamed to tell you, but of course I will. After all, that's why you are here.

CHAPTER 9

Big Mike's - A Girl In Blue

BIG MIKE'S SALOON WAS DIRECTLY across the street from the Mayburn Apartment Building on the north side of Burbank Hill. Next to the saloon towards May Street was an ice cream store and on the corner of the building facing May Street was his son's business, Anthony's Dry Cleaners.

I received quite an education in Big Mike's building. I learned that a saloon still reeks of stale beer, cigarette and cigar smoke early in the morning before it was mopped up and opened for that day's business. I learned at Big Mike's daughter's ice cream store that ice cream was soft before it was chilled and hardened and put into the ice cream cases. And I learned that the Anthony's Dry Cleaning store's steam press made it too uncomfortably hot in the summer to be around but was great comfort in the winter.

Big Mike's property was quite extensive. There were apartments above the saloon and ice cream store, and other apartments above them and the dry cleaners. Big Mike's living area was above his saloon and back towards the alley. In front of his living quarters there was a large common courtyard at the May Street level, with a long hallway connecting his rental apartments with the dry cleaners and May Street itself. There was access to the courtyard by two other pieces of property north of Big Mike's on May Street.

I remember how surprised Mikey had been when I first showed him the view of his Grandpa's building from the top floor of the Mayburn. His Grandfather's building only overlooked May, Burbank and the alley between it and the Pennington Bakery on Boone Street. Whereas my view overlooked just about half of Little Italy and beyond.

When it rained, Mikey and I played indoors. On one of those occasions we happened to be at his dad's dry cleaning shop, so we went next door and played in the hallway. Now Mikey and I had been developing over a period of weeks our theories on how babies were made and only recently came to the conclusion that men put their pee-pees in a woman's hind end. Why it took us so long to understand that was because many of the experts we talked to always sidetracked us with the stork explanation and such. But now, at the age of seven, we finally understood.

Luckily for us an opportunity presented itself with the hallway girl Annie. As usual, when she heard us playing outside her apartment, she came out and sat down in front of her door, with her legs sticking out into the hallway. I guess she felt that if we had to step over her enough times that sooner or later we would have to play with her. Well, she was right, but none of us had ever played that game before or since.

Mikey and I decided to make a baby with Annie. The girl was probably surprised at our sudden appreciation of her presence, and that we even let her play with our toys and sit down on the floor with us. We noticed she had bloomers on under her simple blue dress and that presented a problem. While she played with our toys, we whispered and gestured to each other, "How are we going to do this?"

The hallway didn't seem to be the answer because Mikey's grandparents, parents or the little girl's mother might discover us. Anxiously but quietly, we decided the dry cleaning shop with all its separate and curtained cubicles for laundry, men's shirts, suits and dresses was the best location for privacy. We made certain that no one saw us slip into the shop with the hallway girl. She was fascinated with her first tour of our special hiding places.

You should know that she was much younger than us, at least six months or so. And we knew we were taking advantage of our superior position, knowledge of the terrain, the location and number of the enemy forces and the like. This was going to be a typical Mikey and Jo Jo military campaign.

When we finally found the best location, we signaled that the time had come to act. Who did what to whom first, I can't recall, but immediately the attack began by one of us pulling down her bloomers and unbuttoning our knicker fronts and we both rubbed our pee-pees against the girl's rear end. In three seconds the attack was over. The girl was too surprised to say anything before Mikey and I both ran out the store's side entrance and ran back down the hallway and sat down again on the floor.

The little girl eventually followed and joined us on the floor. We never talked about this to each other all day. The next day, in the quiet of my Grandma's basement, we wondered how long it would take for the hallway girl to have a baby. We both knew it would take longer than a week or two and maybe even a month. Would we become fathers of the same baby? Or would she have two babies? What will our parents say? Would we get a spanking?

With all those unanswered questions, we decided to avoid playing in the hallway for awhile. I don't remember ever seeing the girl in the hallway again. For that matter, Mikey and his parents moved to California shortly afterward and I never saw him again either. I vaguely remember thinking that Mikey's dad knew the little girl's mother pretty well, but I don't remember why I thought that.

Several years ago, when I found myself in Los Angeles on business, I took the time in my hotel room to look for Mikey's name in the telephone directory. I didn't find it. So much for my co-author of "The Girl In Blue" and the co-father of our first baby. Hello, Mikey, wherever you are.

And to the "The Girl in Blue," please forgive our ignorance and trickery. And in your honor, Mikey and I wrote this song:

I'm in love with a girl, A girl in blue.
She's a pretty, pretty girl, The girl in blue.
When I walk down the street I say, "How do?"
She turns around and says, "My, my, it's you."

That is for you Annie and all the other Girls in Blue out there.

CHAPTER 10

Climbing Up Burbank Hill

I DIDN'T REALIZE THE IMPORTANCE of Burbank Street when I lived and played on it. Only that it was a steep climb up Burbank from Boone to May Street and still upward until it finally reached Kenton Street. The working men and women would stride purposefully up the hill, catching their breath only for a second or two at the alleys between streets. Kids like us ran up and down and around it tirelessly, of course, because this was our world and the alleys our playground.

I felt sorry for Grandma and her lady friends because each step was an extra and threatening effort for them. For all the times they uttered, "Please, God, don't let me die climbing this hill," they probably added extra months to their lives because of the exercise. But would they have believed it then? Hell, no.

"Why climb the hill," you ask? Well, if you lived on Symmes Street and you wanted to go to Our Lady Of Mt. Carmel Catholic Church, you had to walk over the Burbank Street Viaduct to Boone Street. Then you had to climb the Burbank Street Hill, past Spider's Cafe, pausing to rest at the alley, then continue climbing again past the entrance to the Mayburn Apartment Building, up to May Street where the Mt. Carmel Church was located. Oh, and you had to cross May Street and climb an additional ten concrete steps to reach the front doors of the church. I guess the little old ladies that did this on a daily basis just offered it up for extra grace in Heaven.

Those of us walking to school each day would continue up Burbank Hill past the church, not pausing a minute at the alley behind it and climb on past One Arm Tony's Saloon to Kenton Street at the very top of the hill.

This is where we kids would split up. If you were going to Windsor Public Grade School, you would cross Kenton Street and continue down the other side on Burbank to the bottom of the hill. Those kids going to Assumption Catholic Grade School would head north on Kenton Street for three blocks to McMillan Street and beyond. High school kids and grownups tried to avoid climbing the Burbank Street Hill as much as possible. Grade school kids like us loved to run up and down the hill every chance we could get, even when we didn't have to. But that was a lifetime ago!

Notice how easily we remember the difficulty of an upward climb, than we do the almost dreamlike and effortless descent down the same hill? Yet I believe it is during the descent of a hill that we pay any notice of our surroundings. Going up we are too busy huffing and puffing to notice much more than the sidewalk beneath our feet, our minds too busy in constant calculations of steps remaining to reach our goal.

That was Burbank Street Hill. You couldn't love it, but you sure could hate going up it. The hill was there and we used it, and after doing so, many cursed it.

CHAPTER 11

The Alleys of Little Italy

THE ALLEYS WERE OUR RELIEF from the mainstream activities of our neighborhood. It was more than just a playground, it was our proving ground as well. The girls would say, "Do you know how to jump rope? You do? Well, how about Double Dutch? Never found a boy yet that can jump Double Dutch." And they were right, I never could.

Still we alley kids became pals anyway. And one by one, the many veils of ignorance were removed from my eyes and my other senses. The children of the alley shared everything. Danny Behan would be happy to give you a knuckle sandwich if you weren't careful. Big Madeline would show you the difference between boys and herself if you were interested, while my friend Tina could show you the latest Jitterbug dance steps the grownups were using down below in Spider's Cafe. It seems I managed to avail myself of all the above at one time or another, and then some.

The Alley was our private playground and we took full advantage of it. We played games of one sort or another all the time. Release was my favorite. Later on, Jitterbugging won out. And we all did a lot of growing up in between.

On Saturday nights especially, Spider's Cafe would be packed with Jitterbug dancers and we would watch them from above, through a window in the alley they would leave open for fresh air. That worked until those of us dancing and singing in the alley became noisier than the people on the dance floor. When that happened, they would close the window on us. We would all moan and groan about it for a while, but then we would go on and do something else.

Zoot Suits and Drape Pants were the latest in men's fashion in those days. I would admire the men dancing below and their Zoot clothes. Bob Dixon had Drape Pants before any of the rest of us kids and what a great Jitterbugger he was. More about Bobby and his Drape Pants later.

CHAPTER 12

Italian Kites - Shot Down Over Goose Neck Hill

ONE DAY A MIXED GROUP of May Street, Boone Street and Alley Kids, ranging in the ages of eight, nine and ten years old, decided to head down Burbank Street, over the bridge to Symmes Street and climb up Goose Neck Hill to play. Years later, WCPO-TV would build a television station and tower on Goose Neck and one of us, Bob Dixon would become a television producer there.

It had rained overnight so it was going to be a little muddy, especially on our secret trails below and along the crest of the hill. But when we got three quarters of the way up our trail, we saw the sight of our lives. There were kites, big and fancy ones flying overhead. They were as beautiful as anything I had ever seen. They were more colorful than any airplane or automobile, and some looked as big as a house.

There were kites shaped like birds and some looked like giant butterflies. They were painted every color of the rainbow. Some were shaped and painted to appear as real birds and others just splashed with colored stripes or rings and all in brilliant hues of red, green, yellow, brown and blue. Wow, what a sight!

I don't recall exactly how it all started, but we began making mud balls from the wet hillside and throwing them up at the kites that were now flying beyond the lip of the hill and over our trail. We could see the kites but not the people flying them. Likewise, the kite pilots couldn't see us below the crest of the hill.

"How dare they fly over our secret trail?" someone said, and we all began making and throwing mud balls at the kites. The first of our missiles fell far short of its mark, but then fate played its role. One of the largest and more beautiful of the kites, the one shaped and colored like an orange butterfly, lost its draft of wind and dropped below the crest of the hill. Someone got a direct hit with a mud ball. And the mud ball didn't pass through it with a clean hole like a machine gun bullet from a Spad into a Fokker. Instead, it ripped a large gaping hole in it and the mud ball was still stuck to the kite's ripped paper material as it fluttered down to the ground towards us.

When the kite's owner came over to the edge of the hill looking for it, he spotted us. He looked older and bigger than us. He started cursing and running toward the top of our trail and down after us. When I got to the bottom of the hill and looked over my shoulder, I saw him catch up to one of my friends and hit him in the back. He fell down but quickly got up and ran until he caught up with the rest of us running back over the Burbank Bridge to Boone Street and safety.

What we didn't realize at the time was that the kite owner didn't just knock my friend down, but actually stabbed him in the back with a pocket knife. Of course, our buddy became an instant hero. When I went home, I didn't intend to tell anyone what had happened. But during dinner I told Momma, Poppa and my sister Anita about my day's adventure. I was probably trying to show off in front of my sister Anita and my parents. You know, Momma asks Poppa how his day was and he replies with, "Nothing special." Then I announce, "I saw a friend stabbed in the back," always trying to be a big shot in my family's eyes and possibly trying to compete with Poppa for some attention.

The next day Momma said the police had come to our third floor apartment looking for me. My buddy's parents had reported the stabbing and the police were looking for witnesses. Mom told them that I had seen the kite owner hit the boy in the back and knock him down, and so the police took my name and said they would get back to us. All my buddies were similarly visited, but it seemed I was the only one to see the actual incident.

A week or so later Mamma and I had to go to the courthouse downtown to tell the judge what happened. I really did feel like a big shot when, after questioning, the judge said I was the star witness to the stabbing. I can't recall what the verdict or punishment was to the kite flyer, or how badly my friend had been wounded because that wasn't important to me. The only thing that mattered to me was the fact that I had been a star witness!

CHAPTER 13

Windsor School and Mt. Carmel Church

AS I'VE MENTIONED EARLIER, my family moved around a lot in those days. But mostly only within Little Italy. We went from Boone Street, across from Spider's and right next to the viaduct to the Mayburn Apartment Building, where my Grandma was janitor. From the third floor of the apartments we moved to the fifth floor. After the twins were born, we moved to a frame house at the bottom of May Street, below Little Goose Neck Hill. Oh yes, there was a Little Goose Neck Hill also. My buddy Danny Orse lived near the top of it.

Throughout these many moves at this time in my life, I managed to continue at Windsor Grade School. I certainly thank God for that blessing. Because, you see, I was able to have Bob Dixon as my best friend and classmate at Windsor School.

Bob and I also played together after school, sang together in the Windsor Chorus and also in the Mt. Carmel Catholic Church Choir. Bob was one of the best friends I ever had. He never asked for anything from me but was always there for me when I needed him. Like the loan of his draped pants with open welt seams that I wore to the eighth grade dance. And much later in life, when he provided some counseling to me, with the help of a bottle of Scotch as I recall, on his boat on the Ohio River.

Bob was the very best at gym class, whatever the sport or exercise. Big as he was compared to the rest of us, he appeared to be seven feet tall, especially to the other Italian kids. I was a head shorter than Bob but a head taller than the rest. We had great times together, and oh dear God, could we harmonize.

Bob sang bass, I sang tenor, Rosella and Tina were altos, Ree Ree and her sister Melina were sopranos. Oh, yes, Bobby Wedding, the smallest kid in school, was a soprano also. Together we sounded terrific and Miss Marsh, our beautiful music teacher, knew it. And do you know, I still *love* that lady to this day?

During the war, Miss Marsh arranged for us to sing at a U.S.O. in downtown Cincinnati. I can remember that even though we were scared stiff, the G.I.s loved us. I'm sure the G.I.s were starved for entertainment, but that excursion did tell us something about ourselves. When the pressure was on, we could perform and perform well. Those performances gave us the self-confidence that we would all rely on later, as you will see.

Every year at Christmas time, the old Windsor Chorus, now in high school, would have a reunion with Miss Marsh and her current crop of singers, and go caroling up and down the streets around Windsor Grade School. She was proud of us and we all loved her. I must confess, however, that it took me years to get over her marrying and becoming <u>Mrs. Connors</u>. Yes, she broke my fifteen year old heart, but I guess I survived.

She would bring her daughter with us when we would go caroling. I think she was a year or two older than we, but I remember being intimidated by her, probably because I was jealous that she was closer to her mother than I was. Weird, huh? I mean, I really idolized that woman!

Miss Marsh was the first person, other than my family, to believe in me. She said I had musical talent. But my parents had other priorities, like trying to feed four children and chose to ignore her comment on my report card: "Joe is musically inclined and should be given an opportunity to play an instrument." To Poppa Nick the only instruments he was interested in were his shears, combs, razors and straps. And for me, the strap was sometimes his instrument of choice, if you get my drift.

Poppa Nick was tall and handsome, and a dead ringer for Maurice Chevalier, especially when he wore his straw kadie hat. Mom loved him, the ladies around Peebles Corner adored him, and everyone he ever met liked him. Even the local Mobsters, his personal customers, liked my Poppa Nick.

Poppa Nick was one of a kind, there's no doubt about it. I only hope that some of him rubs off on my children and theirs. My daughter Nicki reminds me of him quite a bit. I hope that a future grandchild or great grandchild is blessed with the whole Poppa Nick package: looks, personality, dedication and charm. Yes, I would like to see that in my lifetime. Are you listening Lord?

But back to Bob Dixon. I'll never forget that one day he asked, "Where do you and the other kids go on Thursday afternoons?" I answered, "The school allows us to attend our church classes. We go back to Mt. Carmel Church for Sunday School classes. And those of us that are in the Church Choir go upstairs into the church afterward and practice." "Does Rosella, Tina and Ree Ree sing in the choir, too?" he asked. When I replied that they did, he wanted to know if he could come along and sing with us. I said, "Of course." Bob became the best bass voice that Our Lady of Mt. Carmel Church ever heard. His joining us in the choir led to many other wonderful things. We would work the booths at Mt. Carmel's Church Festivals and wash dishes at our Spaghetti and Ravioli Dinners, while we all sang, of course.

In the years that followed, Bob converted to Catholicism, but I didn't have anything to do with that. His mentor and godfather was Charlie LaRich. His joining our church choir enabled us to continue our long-time grade school relationship.

We seemed to have a considerable turnover in assistant priests at Our Lady of Mt. Carmel Church. I guess our tiny, frame church was a good assignment for the newly ordained priests. You know, a Mission without fear of spears, arrows or blow darts. And they were always so young and energetic, fresh out of the seminary.

I can remember a group of us kids being introduced to a newly arrived assistant priest and hearing Father Leonard, our Pastor, tell us all the good things that he expected the new assistant to do for us. We would look at one another, wink and think to ourselves, "here we go again." However, we were quick to get over our juvenile mistrust once we were convinced that they were really serious about trying to help us kids.

What kind of help, you ask? Simply put, we needed a place to play. The politicians would come to our church festivals before every election and always promise our parents a new playground in our neighborhood. And, surprise, surprise, it never happened.

We played in the streets and even on a half block off Boone Street where some houses had been torn down. I mean, we played baseball on top of the bricks, lumber and gravel scattered over the ground. Can you picture some of the weird bounces our baseballs would take? But Meldew (Jerome), the best glove on any team, "ate them up" like he was playing shortstop for the Reds at Crosley Field. What a natural ballplayer Mel was. Oh, by the way, sliding into home plate on bricks and gravel was not highly recommended.

Slowly but surely, between various assistants and our Pastor, Father Leonard, our lives were lifted up from the dull and ordinary to something very special. Our Lady of Mt. Carmel Church already had a great reputation for Spaghetti and Ravioli Dinners, thanks to the ladies of the parish, who prepared and cooked the pasta, the ravioli filling and meatballs. But Fr. Leonard had a surprise for us all. He would introduce a new generation of children at Mt. Carmel to the meaning of "Show Time." More about that later on.

For the record, Father Torta was the first Parish Priest that I recall at Mt. Carmel. He was followed by Father Nardoni and they were both Italian citizens. Father Leonard was the first American-born Pastor assigned to our Parish in my lifetime.

CHAPTER 14

My First Love - Rosella

I BELIEVE I FIRST MET ROSELLA in kindergarten class in the basement of Mt. Carmel Church. My affection for her developed after we moved from the Mayburn to the little frame house at the lower part of May Street. My sister Anita and I would join Rosella and others from Boone and the bottom of May Street walking to Windsor Grade School. Usually we all walked over the Kenton Street Bridge, over Florence Avenue, to Gilbert Avenue and then on up the hill toward Windsor Street and school.

We were in classes together at Windsor for eight years. We played together in gym class and recess and sang together in Miss Marsh's music class and her Windsor Chorus. Those eight years of grade school were the most exciting years of my life and Rosella was my secret love all that time.

Was she a knockdown gorgeous beauty? No. That was a pretty good description of her older sister Mary. Rosella was a solidly built, slightly pixie and freckled faced, pug nosed and bright- eyed girl. Her hair was somewhat strawberry blonde, but not red. And her personality? That was what grabbed me because she was sweet, agreeable, cooperative, harmonious (we sang together), hard working, hard playing and positively wonderful. That folks was Rosella.

I never told Rosella or anybody else how I felt about her. Why? You just don't tell guys or girls that kind of stuff. Certainly not at that time in your life. But she was always very special to me. And I guess I will always remember her as that child. To this day, I can picture her before and after she fell and chipped her two front teeth. To me she will always remain beautiful. Without my realizing it, Rosella has always been the definition of beauty that I compared all others to. I believe that says it all. I was hooked.

Of course, while at school, the boys played with boys and the girls played with girls. But when the opportunity presented itself, like gym classes, recess and lunchtime, we would all play together either in the school yard or ball field. And what a good athlete she was. She could swing a softball bat and throw a ball like a boy and run just as fast. Let me tell you, she <u>was</u> a very special young lady. There will be more about Rosella later on in this writing.

CHAPTER 15

Bob Dixon - Friend and Hero

THERE ARE FEW PEOPLE WE MEET in our lifetime of whom we can say, "He truly changed my life." Whatever my personality was like before I met him, or however smart or decent I may have been, once I met Bob Dixon at Windsor Grade School, my life was altered forever. Bob and I walked to school together. As I said before, we sang in the same Chorus at Windsor, Bob was bass and I sang tenor. I always envied Bobby's deep and earthy voice.

We shared views about everything. The few miles to school passed in a hurry. Bob was bigger and stronger than any of us kids in grade school and he was also very athletic. We were in the same classes together: Mr. Shuster for gym, Miss Marsh for music (we badly wanted them to marry each other) and all the other wonderful teachers we shared for eight great years. The other kids, Joe P-rag, Rosella, Tina, and Ree Ree were all Bob's friends too, but our relationship was very special.

As you know, I had three sisters, but I didn't have a brother. I believe now that I had relegated the duties and honors of brotherhood to Bob. Over our span of years together he unknowingly defined for me, through his own behavior, a high standard which I have tried to emulate. Bob was never aware of the importance his friendship had for me. These are things that neither young boys nor grown men talk about. It's not something you plan. It just happens.

Bob was a natural leader. He would immediately break up fights on the school grounds. When we would choose up sides for softball, he would always make sure that the little kids were included fairly, like little Bobby Wedding. Everyone loved Bob Dixon: the girls, the boys and our teachers. Yes, he was certainly my hero.

One morning, when it was time to walk to school, I went to a neighbor's house and called out to a friend, "Hurry up, it's time to go." His mother stuck her head out of the second floor window and told me that her son wasn't allowed to walk to school with me anymore. I didn't understand because I hadn't done anything to him. In fact, he and I had always been good friends. And I couldn't think of anything I may have done to make his parents mad at me. I was really upset.

Later that night, I told Momma what my friend's mother had said to me. She replied that his mother had talked to her too and that the reason she didn't want him to walk to school with me anymore was because I "walk to school with niggers." She was referring to Bob and his younger sister. I was dumbfounded. This was my first experience with racial bigotry. I was heartsick and couldn't believe what I had just heard Momma say, even if she was just repeating what someone else had said to her.

The next day while walking to school I told Bob what my friend's mother had said. To my surprise, Bob didn't act as upset as I had expected him to be. I asked, "Doesn't that make you mad?" And Bob said, "My mother taught me that white people are going to say things to me, like nigger, but they really don't understand what they are saying." I have never forgotten his most wise response. I don't think we ever talked about that experience again.

When we were told that there would be an eighth grade dance at Windsor School, all I could think of was wanting to look cool. Besides dancing well, there was only one other way to assure that in 1943. The only way to look cool was to wear a pair of Drape pants like Bob wore. The problem was I didn't own a pair of Drapes.

CHAPTER 16

Drape Pants - The Definition of Cool

I WAS VERY UPSET. Our eighth grade dance was Friday afternoon and I didn't have the latest and coolest Drape pants to wear. Pop wouldn't give me the money for them and said, "Only Teutsons (Negroes) wear them anyway." But I just had to have them! I told my buddy, Bob Dixon, of my dilemma and he came up with the solution. "Why don't you borrow a pair of mine?" he said. "They may be a little long for you, but nobody will know the difference." You would have thought he just gave me a million dollars. I was ecstatic!

Bob invited me down to his house to try on a pair. Bob and his sister put on some records and showed me some of their Jitterbug steps. Of course, I begged them both to teach them to me. Oh, I knew how to Jitterbug well enough to get by, but I wasn't satisfied with that. I wanted to be able to move and slide like Bob did, and look as relaxed and smooth as both he and his sister did. I only knew the basics that I had learned in the alley with my sister Anita, Tina and Ann Behan. Bob taught me to relax, feel the music and flow with it. I learned to follow the beat smoothly and with style. I may be out of practice now, but I have never forgotten those special private lessons. Thanks again, Bob!

Believe me, when I walked onto the eighth grade dance floor wearing Bob's beautiful Drape pants, I knew I was cool. The other guys in my class were surprised and I thought, quite envious. But you see, I didn't care what they thought at all. I just wanted to impress one person at that dance, Rosella, and she had no idea I felt that way about her. I planned to ask her to dance with me once I got up my nerve to do so. I wanted this to be the romantic high point of my Windsor School career, but I was scared stiff.

Note: The author has written a three act musical play, "Zoot Alley" devoted to this eighth grade dance.

CHAPTER 17

The Eighth Grade Dance - Sweet Innocence

IN RETROSPECT, WINDSOR GRADE SCHOOL'S dances were typical of all grade school dances. The guys would nervously stand around in groups, clowning around with each other, and the gals would be off to themselves, doing their separate, but just as nervous things. The gals would compliment each other on their dresses, shoes or hairstyles and the guys would mock punch, push or shove each other with both groups keeping a sly eye on one another.

I didn't ask Rosella to dance when I first got there, even though she was the only one I wanted to dance with. Why? Because I was scared to death, that's why. Like the other guys, I had to work myself up to dancing slowly. Rosella and Tina were probably the best girl dancers in class. But I liked Rosella too much to take a chance on her turning me down. You know what I mean? I knew I would die if she said, "No."

So when I finally built up my nerve to start dancing, I asked someone else, Audry, to dance with me. Now Audry was probably the most beautiful girl in the eighth grade, so not knowing my motive, the other guys were real envious of me. Then I danced with Ree Ree. She danced well and we were good friends. Then I danced with Tina, my alley buddy and we looked damn good.

Tina and I had learned to dance in the alley by peeking down through the rear window at Spider's dance floor. Tina was always like a sister to me. Now, I was ready. I had the kinks worked out in my dancing and my nerve built up to finally ask Rosella to dance. Not a slow number! Oh no, I was too nervous for that. But when they put on the next Jitterbug record, I would do it.

Of course, all this time Rosella is dancing with Tina, Bob and other guys. Did Bob know how I felt about Rosella? I don't think anyone knew. This was my big world class secret. I couldn't tell Bob because he played with Joe P-Rag and me, and Rosella is Joe's cousin. If she ever learned how I felt about her, I knew I would die.

The Jitterbug music started and I quickly, but not too boldly, walked over to Rosella and asked her to dance. She smiled and took my hand. We walked out to the dancing area and began dancing. I did not die as I thought I might. I didn't try anything fancy that I could screw up, but we were dancing.

How are we doing? How do we look? Try to relax, I thought. Listen to the beat! Be smooth! Can she tell how nervous I am? Don't mess up! What? It's over? Already? I thanked her for the dance the way grade school kids do and walked her back to Tina. I'm sure Rosella was pleasant because she was always pleasant. It was done. It was over. I could breathe again. I survived. And guess what, folks? I don't think I ever danced with Rosella again. After graduating from Windsor, Rosella went on to Withrow High with a bunch of our grade school classmates.

My family moved away again to the Projects in English Woods on the other side of town, and I was resigned to making new friends there. That only lasted a year and we moved back to Little Italy. I was expected to transfer from Elder Catholic High to Purcell Catholic High. Except for Church activities, the Choir, the Spaghetti/Ravioli Dinners and St. Anthony Festivals and Christmas Caroling at Windsor, our social paths took different directions.

There did come a day of enlightenment, however. Three or four years later, (remember, at that age, three years was a lifetime!) my buddy, Tony Chi, asked me to walk to the bus line at Peebles

Corner where he was to meet his girlfriend Dina Z coming from school. Dina Z lived two houses down from me on Kenton Street and we were pretty good friends, so I went along.

We waited about twenty minutes on Gilbert Avenue for her bus to arrive. When Dina's bus came and the doors opened, I was surprised to see Rosella getting off the bus with her. We all exchanged hello's and started our walk back home to Kenton Street. Tony and Dina were walking together so Rosella and I followed a few steps behind. We talked about our respective schools, but inevitably we reminisced about the good old days at Windsor School. How we missed our teachers, Miss Marsh (Mrs. Connors) and Mr. Shuster, Miss Carr, etc., and the other kids, Bob Dixon and all. It was at this point that she stunned me with a revelation. Rosella said, "You know, in grade school I had the biggest crush on you."

Can you believe it? All those years of my secretly adoring her and now I learned she also had had a crush on me. Sometimes fate can be brutal, and this was one of those times. We talked about our current activities and friends until we finally reached Kenton Street and Dina's house. Dina and Rosella were going to study together, so Tony and I said our goodbyes and we went on to our respective houses. That was my last personal contact with the girl of my *grade school dreams*. Love, respect and good wishes to *you,* Rosella, wherever you are!

CHAPTER 18

A Stranger In Town

BIG MIKE'S ICE CREAM STORE was operated by Big Mike's daughter. Her husband was in the U.S. Army Cavalry. He was one of Michael's heroes. He would come home on leave wearing those split-leather leggings that laced up the front and the two-toned riding britches that they wore in those days and we thought he was a god. We would try and swagger like he did when he walked. And Michael and I always included the cavalry in our war games because Poppa had been a Cavalry man in the Italian Army in World War I. Mom still has his picture, taken after the war in a studio in Rome, standing next to and leaning on a pedestal. She has his medals, too. Yes, he looked like a god, also.

One day we heard that Big Mike's daughter was leaving the Ice Cream Store to join her husband. And before we knew it, the storefront sign was changed to Keller's Ice Cream. A couple of weeks later, a new face joined our seventh grade classes at Windsor Grade School and it belonged to the new operator of the ice cream store's son, Harold Keller.

Harold appeared different from the rest of us. For one thing, he wore better clothes; for another, he seemed to have more money for lunch and things than any of us had. And he was taller, blonde and blue-eyed and most of us were not. He was not Italian. In fact, he was from Kentucky, around Louisville, I believe.

The girls, Tina, Rosella and others, seemed to be attracted to him and that bothered me some. But after playing around the neighborhood together that summer, I began to like him, too. The free ice cream cones his dad or mom would give me when I was with Harold helped me to accept him a lot quicker than I would have otherwise, I do believe. Did I mention that he wore a gold watch? Oh yes, that was Harold. And at some point during our summer before eighth grade, Harold told me he liked Tina a lot.

Now Tina's dad owned Louie's Pool Room on Boone Street next door to Spider's Café. Tina and her family lived above the Pool Room with its main entrance on the alley across from the Mayburn Apartment Building. Harold learned that the alley was our only playground for hide and seek, jump rope, hop scotch, and release. Where we had all learned to jitterbug and say new dirty words. Where we could talk about things you would not talk about with your parents or other grown-ups. Where we developed our early opinions and even had some arguments and an occasional fight. All the above while peeking into the back of Spider's Café's dance floor from the alley above. Harold became smitten with our world as well as with Tina.

Grandma's garbage cans for the apartment building were out there in the alley, too. And yes, the stench of the garbage cans could become a little much at times. The Behans lived across from Grandma's basement apartment on the corner of the alley and Burbank Street. After school, Ann Behan, who was fifteen years old, helped Momma take care of my twin sisters. We didn't call her a babysitter in those days. The Cioffis, a large family with boys and girls, lived further down the alley, but their main entrance fronted on Boone Street. All the houses on the west side of May Street had access to the alley as did all the houses on the east side of Boone Street. It was also my short cut to the back of Jo Jo's house next door when we walked to Windsor School together.

Harold wanted to become one of us alley kids. His problem was that he had too many material things that we didn't have and therefore, he did not qualify. I guess you could say that we had a closed club. However, that didn't change the way he felt about Tina.

CHAPTER 19

My First Date - Unforgettable

YES, HAROLD LIKED TINA a lot. However, so did an "uptowner" and his name was Miles Randsom (as in handsome). His daddy owned a beverage bottling company on Florence Avenue. One day he approached me with a proposition, "Why don't we take Tina and Rosella to a Cincinnati Reds ball game?" Well, in the first place, I had never taken a girl, other than my sister Anita, anywhere and, in the second place, I didn't think I had the nerve to ask Rosella.

Tina and I always played together with the other alley kids, so asking her was easy. But it would be impossible for me to ask Rosella to go because she might refuse me. And as I have already confided in you, but not to Miles, she was the secret love of my life. Miles said, "Maybe we can ask Tina to talk to Rosella?" I thought that scheme might work and so I agreed to talk to Tina about it.

Of course, there was another problem. I needed sufficient money to pay the expenses for two people going to a Cincinnati Reds ball game. So before I talked to Tina, I asked Momma if it would be okay. She said that she would talk to Poppa Nick if the girls agreed to go. Tina agreed and talked to Rosella and she said, "Yes." Both of their parents approved of the outing also. I don't know how difficult it had been for them to get their parents permission, but my Poppa thought we were all "pottsa" (crazy). Of course, Miles had no problem at all.

Poppa Nick toyed with me before he gave me the five dollars Miles and I figured we needed to cover expenses. Like, "OK, OK, I'll give you two dollars, that should be plenty." "No? OK, I'll give you three dollars," to which Momma said, "Nick, quit teasing and give him the five dollars he needs. It's your son's first date."

He gave me the money but still thought I was pottsa. My filial initiation over, I felt like I was ten feet tall. Can you imagine how excited I was? Rosella and me on a date? Wow!

Sunday finally arrived, and the four of us headed for Crosley Field and the baseball games. Did I mention yet that it was a double header? On our walk up to McMillan Street and the street car line, Miles suggested to me that I let him hold all our money. Never having gone on a date before, and being very unsure of myself, I agreed and gave him my five dollars.

We boarded the crosstown street car. The two girls and I walked back to our seats while Miles paid the conductor and got our transfers. At the bottom of McMillan Hill, we transferred to another street car going towards Downtown from Camp Washington. When we got off the streetcar at Crosley Field, it was like we were in a different world. People were coming from all directions and all heading for the lines in front of the ticket windows and gates.

Now I had been to Knothole Ballgames before, where we just walked up to the main gate and showed the attendant our Knothole cards and were directed to sit in the bleachers. But this was a Sunday doubleheader and we were going to buy the best general admission seats we could get. Miles bought our tickets, while Rosella, Tina and I had fun people watching.

There was the peanut vendor roasting his peanuts right there in front of everyone, with a large umbrella over him and his cooker.

There were people of all ages and modes of dress. Men in straw kaddies and women in flat straw hats to protect them from the sun. The noise people made out on the street before they were even in the ball park was a shock to me. When Miles came back with our tickets, we made our way through the gate and we were ushered to our seats.

I was always amazed to see the brilliant green grass of Crosley Field. I guess that was to be expected when you live in a park-less neighborhood like we did. The brightness of the field did tricks with my eyes, causing me to squint and refocus for a minute or so. I think the word "dazzling" must have originated at Crosley Field on that bright and beautiful double header Sunday.

After a few innings of baseball, someone suggested a soft drink so Miles and I headed for the vendor's stand. That's where Harold discovered that he had lost his wallet. I was shocked and couldn't believe it. We backtracked our route from the gate and ticket window, but didn't find it.

We asked the ticket taker if he had seen the wallet, but we had no luck there either. We finally reported it to a policeman and headed back to our seats. We didn't know what or how we were going to tell Tina and Rosella.

We probably had spent three innings looking for the lost wallet.

The girls had to be wondering what happened to us. I didn't know or care who was winning the ball game, I just wanted to crawl out of my skin and disappear. My humiliation weighed a ton and my heart was broken. Yet we said nothing to the girls.

The first game was over and we still didn't offer to get refreshments. The second game was half over before someone, somehow, managed to bring up the subject of Coca Colas and hot dogs. Thank God the ice was broken. Finally released from our stupid silence, we confessed our folly to the girls.

Naturally, the girls were wonderful. They had guessed something like that had happened but waited patiently for the truth to come out. You can imagine how hungry and thirsty four thirteen year olds were by the seventh inning of the second ball game of a double header. They suggested we pull all our meager resources together and see how much we had to work with. Rosella had some change, Tina had a street car ticket good for one ride, and Miles and I had some coins also. No, we didn't give our change to Miles to hold for us!

We calculated that with Tina's ticket we had enough money to pay for the Mount Adams Incline ride up to Eden Park. From there, it was about a one hour walk to Little Italy and home.

But there was a much bigger problem with our plan. We faced an unknown length of miles to walk from Crosley Field through downtown Cincinnati before we could reach the base of the Mount Adams Incline, far below Eden Park. And how long would it take us to walk there? No one could tell us. Someone did suggest the best route to take to get Downtown. We knew that once Downtown, we could find our way to the Incline.

After the second ball game ended, we exited Crosley Field and walked with the crowd toward the business district Downtown. Yes, there was safety in numbers, but we really didn't fear for ourselves. That wasn't because we were young, foolish or ignorant of the possible dangers involved, but because at that time, that area of town, the West End, was still residential. Like our own neighborhood, there were people sitting outside their houses and apartments, on their steps or on kitchen chairs. We didn't know then how quickly all that would change. We had never heard the term Urban Renewal.

When we finally arrived Downtown, the girls had fun window shopping at the department stores we passed. There was Shillito's, Pogue's and McAlpin's, the movie theaters, tailor shops, dress shops, jewelry and shoe stores on our route. Of course, it hurt to see all the restaurants we couldn't afford to go into, or the novelty shops that we would have to pass by. However, we did take advantage of Fountain Square's public restrooms and water fountains before we continued our hike to the bottom of Mt. Adams Hill and the Incline.

I must confess that we did not walk briskly toward our destination, the Incline. We took a steady but sometimes leisurely path through the Downtown area. Tina and Rosella were enjoying the displayed women's fashions and making the most of our calamity, and we really had some fun.

Finally reaching the Incline, we traded our meager collection of coins and Tina's one street car ticket for four one-way tickets. They didn't allow pedestrians to board the Incline platform until the next streetcar arrived and was safely boarded. There were several other people waiting with us. Finally, the familiar Number 49, the ZOO - EDEN streetcar turned off Broadway Avenue and motored right onto the Incline's platform.

Boarding a streetcar onto the platform is a two man operation. While the conductor stays at the controls, a second man, usually the Incline attendant, must disengage the rear twin trolley poles from the regular overhead electric lines and secure them flat against the roof for the ride up the Incline. Once the

Incline platform reaches the top of the hill, a similar procedure is followed to reconnect the electric lines. After Number 49 was maneuvered onto the platform, we pedestrians were allowed onto the platform and together, man and machine, we were lifted up to the top of Mt. Adams.

I have often wondered what my thoughts were that early evening as we were lifted from our adventure through Downtown to the relative security of Mt. Adams and Eden Park, so close to Little Italy. Unfortunately, those memories deserted me a long time ago. At best, the panorama of Cincinnati's skyline, the winding Ohio River and the surrounding hills of southern Ohio and northern Kentucky, beautiful and breathtaking as they are, were only a bittersweet respite for me before the final chapter of this day was played out.

I was heartbroken over the lasting impression that this day would obviously leave with Rosella. The better part of our situation, the adventurous hike through Downtown Cincinnati with my secret love, was at an end. Did the pain in my heart show through? Was I even civil toward Miles? Will I ever forgive myself for being stupid enough to give him all my money in the first place? If this is what my first date is like, will I ever allow myself a second one?

On the other hand, I was Poppa Nick's only son and I had some of his bullshit bravado that would be displayed much later when I was in high school. But that wasn't me brooding over my lost opportunity for pure love on that warm summer night in 1942. Did I smile through it all? Or was I silent and withdrawn as I was to become only too soon? I had better move on here before I get ahead of my story.

We walked off the Incline's platform onto Mt. Adams and began the final segment of our trip along the paths of Eden Park toward home. A different sort of an adventure was about to occur. By this time, we are singing school songs as we walked along the park's paths, happy to have reached familiar territory. I should mention that it was now about 8:30 P.M. by Miles' gold watch, and we still had about an hour's walk before we reached home.

Tina and Miles were strolling along behind Rosella and me. They didn't seem to show the same urgency to move along quickly that I did. Suddenly they decided to sit on a bench. The next thing I knew and without any warning from Miles they were kissing. "What the heck is going on here?" I asked myself.

I was embarrassed because I didn't have the nerve to kiss Rosella, especially after that day's fiasco. Did I even hold her hand? Wasn't there even a spark of the male fires that were so soon to control me? "Don't you think we better keep going," I asked? I don't believe Tina and Miles appreciated my concern, but they did join Rosella and me as we picked up the pace toward home.

Enough of the second guessing about what I may have said or what Rosella, Tina, Miles and I may have been thinking as we made our way through Eden Park and out onto Gilbert Avenue and the Kenton Street Bridge. We walked over the bridge and separated at May Street. Miles walked Tina back to Burbank and I walked Rosella to her house on Boone.

Rosella's house had an iron fence separating their front courtyard from the sidewalk. When we approached her house, we saw that her whole family was outside sitting in the courtyard. "Where in the hell have you been?" her dad shouted. "Don't you know it's almost ten o'clock?"

Rosella explained to them what had happened. I honestly don't remember if I uttered a word or, for that matter, was the brunt of more chastisement. I remember leaving her courtyard and walking the final ten thousand miles home. The point I'm making is this. That was the longest three block walk of my life. Because I knew that when I got home, I would have to go through the whole explanation one more time for Momma and Poppa Nick. "Where in the hell have you been?"

Of course, I can't remember what my parents said or how I replied to them, and what Poppa Nick's last word to me was. All I can remember, and for all of the years since, is the look on Rosella's dad's face and his question, "Where in the hell have you been?" Something inside me died that night. Was it innocence? I'm not sure, but with the disaster at the ball park, the humiliation when we confessed the lost money to Rosella and Tina and finally, the absolute destruction of any ounce of self-assurance I may have managed to retain before reaching Rosella's courtyard, I bade my world goodbye.

I would never speak about this to others again. I would never seek out Rosella to talk, to play, to sing again. I felt I could never look her straight in the eyes again. I never dated anyone else in Little Italy either. That world was shattered for me. In a sense, I had black-balled myself for life.

I knew that I would have to relive that infamous Sunday again when I sat down to write these remembrances; but I assure you, I didn't realize how painful it still remains. Please forgive me, Rosella, wherever you are.

CHAPTER 20

Tony Wass - My High School Buddy

I DIDN'T GET TO KNOW Tony Wass very well until we moved back to Little Italy from English Woods. The reason? Wass went to the Assumption Catholic Grade School and I went to Windsor Public Grade School. Oh, I would see him around church or selling papers but we weren't very close at the time. We became super good friends, practically inseparable, after we both found ourselves in the same freshman class at Purcell Catholic High School. Tony and I would ride the same streetcars to and from school. Sometimes we walked the five miles home from school together, especially if they had pumpkin pie for lunch and I spent my carfare on an extra piece. Pumpkin pie is my all time favorite dessert. Tony and I would talk about everything: the War (WW II), the world, politics, religion, movies, sports, but nothing took priority over girls, our most favorite subject. Ah, those hormones.

Tony and I were in the same class together because I flunked my first freshman year in high school (1943) and joined him during my second tour of duty. Yes, I had a discipline problem. A bit of rebellion that went astray. Why the rebellion? I had better explain.

I didn't know then, but I do believe now, that I felt uprooted when we left Little Italy for English Woods. I was powerless to do anything about it. My anger was suppressed for a time because I was allowed to complete my last few months in eighth grade at good old Windsor School. In the fall, my grade school friends went on to other Catholic, public or commercial high schools in and around Walnut Hills, but I was stranded fifteen miles away in English Woods and had to attend Elder Catholic High School with strangers. I really didn't like that at all, but I did try to make the best of it. However, those suppressed feelings would emerge again later, and I would have to pay the consequences.

I met some great guys and gals in the Projects and I was somewhat reconciled to my situation. But then it happened again. For reasons I refused to understand at the time, my parents decided to move back to Little Italy. The long series of bus rides to streetcar and transferring to yet another streetcar proved to be too much for Poppa Nick. Getting to his barber shop sometimes took over an hour.

Think about it, he closes the shop at 6:00 P.M., finishes up his last customers (another half hour?), sweeps the floor and starts his trip home. My guess is Poppa Nick would get home for dinner around 8:00 P.M. each day. When you have been on your feet all day, as barbers are, that final long walk up the hill from the bus line had to be a killer. But at the time that didn't mean a damn thing to me. I was only into Me, Me, Me at the time. After all, I was fourteen years old. Don't I have a vote?

If you're thinking, "But you got to go back with your old friends. Wasn't that what you wanted?" the answer is Yes and No. My new friends had convinced me to go to Elder Catholic High School with them and I did for six weeks. I got caught up in all the football hoopla and the new school spirit thing. Can you remember what that was like? And here I am back in my old neighborhood all right but transferred to yet another Catholic school, Purcell High. Which just happens to be the football rival of my first school, Elder High. See what I mean?

By the way, it was probably my choice to go to Purcell. I'm sure Poppa Nick would have preferred not having to pay my tuition and would have loved to have me go to Withrow, a public high school. But it couldn't be the same now. My graduating grade school friends had already moved on. Some of them were at

Purcell but not Bob Dixon, Rosella or Tina. These were my lifelong friends.

And another relevant point, I believe, was the fact that I had spent a good portion of my eighth grade year at Windsor saying goodbye forever to all these people. "And now he's back," they may have asked? "Boy, what a bullshiter he is," they probably thought. Am I still feeling sorry for myself after all these years, you ask? Of course, I am.

Now couple my attitude at the time with, one: a hostile and sometimes belligerent relationship with my teachers and fellow students, and two: my playing hooky for twenty one straight days in May, and I believe you can see why I had to repeat my freshman year at Purcell? Yes I was wrong, but that was what happened.

Now Tony Wass was born in Italy, and his Poppa, like mine, had a very heavy Italian accent. Come to think of it, all of our parents, except my Momma, had accents. I bring that up to explain why my friends, both Tonys, Frank and Joe could speak Italian so much better than I could. At Tony's house, Italian was the only language spoken. Whereas, at my house Pop would only speak Italian when he cursed or didn't want us kids to know what he and Mom were talking about. Surprise, surprise, folks! We kids knew more than they thought we did, yes siree.

When we moved back to Little Italy, we lived on Kenton Street, three doors up from Morgan Avenue and two blocks south of McMillan. Some would say that put us on the northeastern fringe of Little Italy, even though we were only two blocks away from Burbank. The old single story, frame house we lived in is just an empty parking lot now, but in those days we kept it as busy as Grand Central Station. My buddies hung out there, my sister and her girlfriends were usually around somewhere, trying to listen in to our bull sessions, and of course, all of us were hungry. Remember Mom?

CHAPTER 21

The Dime Store

ONE HOLIDAY SEASON, TONY WASS and I got part time jobs at Woolworth's Dime Store on McMillan Street near Peebles Corner. We worked in the basement mostly, opening boxes of supplies and then delivering the different items upstairs to the proper sales counters. Did I mention that there were a lot of high schools girls working there also? One of the girls, Millie, I had met and danced with at a Regina High School dance. So naturally she and I got to know each other better. Tony, at the same time, met and became friends with Betty Jo, who worked across McMillan Street from the dime store. Millie worked at the notions counter and she and Betty Jo became friends. Believe me, both girls were beautiful.

Millie was taller than Betty Joe and I was taller than Tony, so we all kind of matched up pretty well. Hey, appearances were damn important when you were seventeen. I would find any excuse to deliver supplies to the notions counter. Eventually, we arranged a double date with Millie and Betty Jo. Or was it Betty Jo and Millie who decided to date us? Hell, we will never know the answer to that question. Anyway, after that first double date together, the four of us became very tight, so to speak. We would go to the movies together, to the Sunbeam Restaurant together, Graeter's Ice Cream store together. In a word, we became inseparable.

After a holiday season of work at Woolworth's, which was more like fun and games to us, we basically paired off. Now our romances began to flourish. We would still double-date a lot, but we kind of went our separate ways when it came to making out. The definition of making out in 1947 was, I am sure, a helluva lot different then than it is today. We necked and we petted (Oh yes!), but I was dumb as hell about how to move on to the next level. Get the picture? In other words, I wanted to do the wrong thing, but in the right way.

You see, I was convinced that Millie was a virgin and that scared the hell out of me. Worse yet, she was convinced that I knew how to make it happen. And she basically left it up to me to get us both through this training period. Holy shit, what a heavy responsibility. This was certainly new territory for me. I really didn't want to be the first guy to do this to her. But when I was with Millie, reason seldom won out. There was this overpowering physical attraction that I couldn't overcome. Even when we argued, if she reached out and touched my hand, I would melt. And she knew it, too. She was to use this power over me, time after time, again and again. "Is this what love is?" I would ask myself. I truly didn't know the answer, but I was certainly under the spell of love's physical gifts.

Tony and I still hung out at Frisco's Bowling Alley with the guys, only now, Betty Joe and Millie would come to watch us bowl. And after we were finished bowling, instead of going next door to Mac's for a hamburger with the guys, Tony and I would bring the girls along. This routine soon became a pain-in-the-ass to the other guys. So Tony and I started taking the girls across Gilbert Avenue to the Sunbeam Restaurant every week. Jimmy the Greek, the manager, got to know the four of us very well. And the Sunbeam Restaurant became our special place.

Invariably, I would order the ham, egg, American cheese, lettuce and tomato double-decker with mayo. It became for Jimmy and me, "the usual." After eating, the couples, Betty Jo and Tony, Millie and I would go our separate ways. Betty Jo only lived about a mile down Gilbert Avenue toward town, but Millie lived a long street car or bus ride away in Norwood. And once we got to Norwood, we still had a mile to walk from the street car line to Millie's house. There were times when it was real late that Millie would go home alone. For me, a round trip took at least two hours.

When we were in school, I could only take her home on weekend nights. Millie was very understanding and practical about that. Her good Zinzinnati German upbringing, I suppose. Of course there were exceptions to this drill. Occasionally a friend with a car would offer to drive us to Norwood. And there were other times when the dictations of the heart had to be considered. What great adventures those trips turned out to be.

CHAPTER 22

Frank - Trumpeter of the Band

LIKE TONY, I GOT TO know Frank real well after we moved back to Little Italy from English Woods. I had known Frank from Mt. Carmel Church and we had sold papers together when we were in grade school. But Frank was almost two years older than I. He was a sophomore when I was a freshman (the first time) and he played trumpet in our little (and pathetic when compared to public schools) Purcell High School Band.

Frank would go to school with Tony and me, but when there, he would hang out with an older group of guys. We were always impressed with Frank's serious scholastic drive. Frank had visions of becoming an electrical engineer some day. One of his part time jobs while in high school was working at the electric repair shop next door to Heineman's Grocery Store on May Street. We all thought that Frank was the smartest in our group. Our criteria for that exalted position was as follows: 1) how much you knew about girls, 2) how much personal experience you had with girls, and 3) knowing best where to pick up girls. Ah, did you notice that it had nothing to do with academics?

Have I convinced you by now that girls were very important to us? Ok! Very important, yes, but girls had to fight for the top spot in priority with us. And their competition was formidable. Our most important pastime, the highest priority and our most favorite activity was SPORTS. Believe me, nothing took precedence over sports with us. We played C.Y.O. (Catholic Youth Organization) softball in the summer and basketball in the winter.

In the fall and winter we played choose-up sides, touch football (two hand tag) in the streets and tackle football at Triangle Park on Taft and Reading Road whenever we had a holiday or Catholic Holy Day and didn't have to go to school. We had all started bowling in the Mt. Carmel Bowling League at Frisco's. As we improved, we bowled for Benny's Bar and later, for my favorite beer, Hudepohl, also at Frisco's Lanes. Frank, Tony D'Ang and I also bowled in the Purcell High School League at Mergards Lanes.

What did we do between or after these sports activities, you may ask? We shot pool, of course. Frisco's and Mergards both had great pool halls, or billiard rooms as they would prefer to be called. And we availed ourselves of the plush green felt tables every chance we got.

Shooting pool was both an art and a science. Geometry is the key to planning a shot, tactical science is required in the selection of a shot, and skill is vital in making each shot. Art comes into play when you build the drama of the game to an exciting climax. And each shooter had his own style (art again). But when someone knocks the nine ball in the pocket on the break in a game of Nine Ball, that my friends, is pure luck. Oh yes, there is another ingredient usually present in pool halls that I forgot to mention, and that is gambling. Besides art, science, skill and luck, gambling brings to pool the sleeze and pressures of greed, and we loved every minute of it. Not that we were very successful. On the contrary, we usually lost our asses, but we did manage to do it with style. You see, art wins out again.

CHAPTER 23

Joe Al - Our Mr. Muscles

ABOUT A HALF BLOCK UP Kenton Street from our house lived another guy in our group, Joe Al. Built square to the ground, and big enough in the arms to show-off by rolling up his sleeves most of the time, Joe was our happy-go-lucky muscle man. Wow, could he laugh at a joke. Ironically, that's why Joe couldn't tell a joke. He would start laughing in the middle of his telling and never make it to the punch line. It makes me smile just thinking about him.

Joe went to Assumption Grade School with Frank. Joe had sold newspapers with the rest of us, so we knew each other somewhat before I moved away to English Woods. When we moved back to Little Italy, to Kenton Street, Joe and I became much better acquainted. Right around the corner from Joe, on Wayne Street, is where Frank lived. Frank and Joe had been close friends for years.

Because of our close proximity to one another, the three of us started hanging out together. We would play street baseball in front of Frank's house on Wayne Street and courtyard basketball over at Chicken Lynch's house on May Street. We called it Chicken Lynch because they had a poultry business behind their house. The Lynch kids all went to Assumption School and Church, so Frank and Joe had to introduce me to them. I was one of the outsiders who went to public school.

A couple houses down from the Lynch's lived the Dickhouses. Again, these kids all went to Assumption Grade School and church, but like Franky and me, they also went to Purcell High School. I had seen them around but didn't know them too well. Let me mention here that Purcell was a Catholic boys school. Most of my buddies had sisters, of course, and they went to either Regina (Catholic) High School for girls, Withrow (Public) High School or a commercial school. So my sister Anita became good friends with the Regina Gals as I did with the Purcell Guys.

CHAPTER 24

Chicken Lynch

THE LYNCHES HAD A BASKETBALL HOOP attached to their back building, which was the chicken processing plant. There was no backboard, so if you went in for a fast lay-up shot, you invariably slammed into the sheet metal building. Our basketball court was the thirty feet or so of concrete between the back door of the Lynch house and the back building. The iron fence along the May Street sidewalk and their next door neighbor's fence were our out-of-bounds markers.

We played basketball at Lynch's almost every day after school. Paul Lynch was closest to us in age and he owned the hoop and the basketball. Do you realize the power this gave him? Not that Paul ever took advantage of us because that wasn't his way, but he certainly was very important to us. Come to think of it, Paul could dribble better than any of us, he could shoot better than us, and he could fake us out-of-our-socks any time he wanted to. So maybe there was some taking advantage going on, but guess what, folks, we all loved it and in the process, we really got turned-on to basketball.

Now, the Lynch boys and the Dickhouse boys played organized basketball at Assumption Church and also had a team in the C.Y.O. (Catholic Youth Organization) League. It was about this time that Franky, Joe, Tony Wass and Tony D'Ang and I, along with other guys in the neighborhood, Meldew, Andee and his brother Joe P-Rag, decided to get a basketball team of our own. To do that meant getting the Mt. Carmel Parish Priest, Father Leonard, to sponsor us in the C.Y.O League, which of course he did upon request.

He probably received pay-back from us, like serving 6:30 A.M. Mass or cleaning up the church basement periodically. The Our Lady of Mt. Carmel Basketball Team was something to behold. We were the most raggedy looking bunch of kids that ever walked onto a basketball court. And probably the smallest in height ever seen in the C.Y.O. League. Remember, we were from Little Italy and most of us were considerably shorter than our Teutonic neighbors.

Ability had nothing to do with who got to play. Hell, we were lucky to have one or two extra players each week, besides the basic five needed to put a team on the floor. And there were times when only four people showed up and we had to forfeit the game. When that happened, the other team would furnish us a player and we would still play a game before returning home. But we did play and lose. And play again and lose. And finally play again and win. It was wonderful.

We would go into a big parish to play and they would have smart looking uniforms, and many more basketballs than the one or two we had. They had teams of ten to fifteen players. They usually had full basketball courts, whereas we didn't even have a court for a while. We would practice in our church basement, but we couldn't shoot jump or long shots because the ceiling was too low. Yet we did get better organized, we did learn to play basketball with the best of teams and most importantly, we had a hell of a lot of fun. Remember, folks, no television - this was it for entertainment.

There was one parish, St. John's downtown on Vine Street, that gave its basketball team a unique home court advantage. Their basketball court floor was slanted downhill toward their stage. You had to run up to one end of the court and basket and down to the other. The basketball court was used as a theater to seat people for their annual and famous Passion Play during Lent. I always got a special kick playing there.

There were other strange courts, like St. Cecelia's, near Roger Bacon High School. They actually had fat pillars down the sides of their court because it was the basement of their church. Oh, that brings back painful memories to me. Not because I ever ran into one of the pillars, but I just remembered how very good their teams were and how they always beat the hell out of us. We did improve with time thanks to the young assistant priest, who Father Leonard had put in charge of us. We even got uniforms and more basketballs.

His involvement led to other sports and activities. We had a Mt. Carmel C.Y.O. softball team. Did I already mentioned the Mt. Carmel Bowling League (about six teams)? And finally, we got our own Activity Hall where we could shoot some medium size jump shots but still no long two hand set shots.

CHAPTER 25

Charlie Ritchie - Our Swaggering Sailor

CHARLIE RICHIE, AS YOU CAN guess by his name, was the only Irish member of our little band. Rich, as we called him, lived on Symmes Street on the other side of the Burbank bridge. A fringe part of Little Italy, Symmes Street begins to break up the Italian influence that the viaduct seems to have assigned to the Boone Street side. Rich wasn't Catholic, so he wasn't part of our life at Mt. Carmel Church nor at Purcell High School. Like the rest of us, he just wanted to be a part of something, and our group was what he found himself with.

Like Frank and Joe Al, Richie was a year or two older than Tony Wass and myself and three years older than Tony D'Ang. That pretty much explains the pecking order in the group. Because of his maturity, Rich had a very earthy influence on us. We saw him as a man of the world especially when he was old enough to join the Navy while the rest of us had to go to school. It made us feel like babies when he did that, and it totally destroyed my ego to see him in his uniform whenever he was on furlough. The war was over in 1946, but sixteen and seventeen year olds like us were pissed off that we missed it. And we were doubly pissed off that he wore that great looking Navy uniform and we had to wear a shirt and tie to school everyday.

CHAPTER 26

Peebles Corner - Like Broadway and 42nd Street.

LIKE OTHERS BEFORE AND AFTER US, our gang was very territorial, but only in the sense that we always bummed around Peebles Corner. We never fought with other gangs or anything like that. Hell, we were lovers, not fighters. We just loved the action around Peebles Corner.

We bowled at Frisco's Bowling Alley almost exclusively. Occasionally, we bowled at Mergards Bowling Lanes, but it was six blocks further east on McMillan from Peebles Corner. Besides, Mergards was newer, had more lanes on one floor and it had that new soundproof ceiling that deadened the impact noise when the bowling ball struck the ten pins. And who in the hell would want that? Tony Wass and I thought that it was a bit too snobbish for our taste.

As I had said, we would shoot pool at Frisco's as well. Many times we bowled or shot pool until they closed the place. We would say, "Just one more game of nine ball, O.K.? Please? We will cover all the tables for you." Yes, each table had a heavy "table cloth" that was put on at closing time. And usually, we would be allowed to play one more game.

All of us paperboys would pick up our papers on the eastern side of the Corner, on Gilbert Avenue, in front of the Sunbeam Restaurant. We sold papers all around Peebles Corner because none of us had a specific corner assigned to us. Only the older boys and men, like Little Louis who played drums at One Arm Tony's on weekends, had an intersection corner of his very own at McMillan and Kemper Lane.

It had to look strange as hell to see three or four kids with the same papers under their arms walking and hawking down McMillan Street trying to beat each other to the next oncoming potential customer. But we really didn't care how many papers we sold. We were just working our way down to the Hotel Alms, where the WKRC Radio Station was located, so we could play king of the hill behind the White Tower hamburger shop. Priorities, yes we always had our priorities.

And we would sing a lot; "Dream" was our favorite - "when you're feeling blue, dream, that's the thing to do." One night at Frank's house we were all up in his room on the second floor and it was hot as hell. Frank played "Dream" on his trumpet and the rest of us sang the lyrics. Someone would get mad at someone else for being off key or Frank would blow a clunker note and we would all laugh like hell. Of course, big shot here, I would be trying to harmonize and I would screw up, too. I was the only one in our gang that sang in the Mt. Carmel Church Choir and the Windsor Glee Club. Singing was one of my few strong suits. Folks, we had a great time that night and it was for me unforgettable.

CHAPTER 27

Our Corner - Hanging Out

POPPA NICK WOULD GET DAMN angry with me if I wasn't home by 11:00 P.M. on school nights. Sometimes he would come out looking for me and he knew where to look because my buddies and I would usually be shooting the bull on the corner of Kenton and Wayne Streets. This is when we lived on Kenton Street and I was going to Purcell High School.

Like other guys before and after us, we would sit on the cement steps of the corner house and talk about sports, girls, life, girls, music, girls, etc. Hell, you probably did it too? I mean, we all did it. The only difference about us is that we used a corner that allowed Frank to see his house, Joe A. to see his and me to see mine. Tony D'Ang didn't mind being five blocks from his home because as we all discovered later, he could keep an eye on Millie Fee's house up Wayne Street.

We also learned later that on many of those nights we spent talking about girls and other things, my sister Anita, Cheri and Millie watched and listened to us from Millie's house across the street on Wayne. We didn't realize we were so loud. Hell, they heard all our secrets. Poor Tony D'Ang, he didn't realize (none of us did) how organized and sneaky girls were in intelligence gathering. Maybe we should have a Girls Intelligence Agency instead of a CIA. I don't think the enemy would stand a chance, just as Tony, Millie's target, didn't.

The stuff they must have heard us talk about. I wonder if they heard us talk about how we can piss over a car by holding back as you build up pressure in your penis and then letting go in one big burst. Most boy child parents can relate to that. Boy babies do that every now and then, don't they? Even baby sitters have experienced that sudden shower on occasion.

As inexperienced as we were, we naturally discussed lovemaking a lot. Like who we thought did it and who didn't. This would eventually lead to which of us had the biggest cock. We all knew that no one on earth had one like Red A's from Boone Street. We all heard about his bet in Louie's Pool Room, that his cock would span the width of the toilet bowl and damn if it didn't.

Another favorite spot was a block farther up Kenton Street where it meets and ends at McMillan Street. The Dog Patch Bar was there on the southeast corner. And their ladies room had a blackened window that faced on to Kenton Street. Unknown to all but ourselves, there was a little peep hole scratched through the paint in the lower half of the window. We would bullshit on the sidewalk and keep checking until someone would go in. Then we would push and shove each other to curses of, "My turn, damnit, my turn."

I can still see that unsuspecting blonde hillbilly girl who lived across Kenton Street from the bar. There she was, straddling the toilet, singing along with the music coming from inside the bar and ignoring completely the piss drizzling down her legs. That was one of the funniest sights we ever saw, and it is the only thing I can still remember about our secret window. So much for the many mysteries we expected to have uncovered by that chance scratch of paint.

Every once in a while a cop would come by and tell us to move on, but we would come right back after awhile. However, not if the cop was Big Mike. Big Mike was a tall, strong Irish cop. What other kind was there? When he said move, you can bet we moved. Even Pop who was friendly with everyone was exceptionally so with Big Mike. Around Peebles Corner Mike was the law, and we respected him because he didn't take any bullshit from anyone.

Once the manager of Dow Drugs Store, on the northwest corner of Peebles, complained to Mike about all the people blocking his entrance. They were streetcar commuters who ran under the drug store's awning for protection from the rain. Big Mike, wearing his black policeman's rain slicker, would tell them, "Don't block the entrance," but he would never tell the commuters to get back into the rain. That's the kind of law I grew up with and miss so much today.

Which reminds me, my friend Joe Al sold newspapers on that corner. One day, he and Tony Wass were horsing around when "CRASH," Joe ended up going right through the drug store's plate glass window. Luckily no one got hurt, but we teased Joe and Tony about it for years. I can't remember if Joe lost his newspaper corner over that or not. Where was Big Mike the policeman that day?

Peebles Corner was to us what Broadway and 42nd Street was to New Yorkers. Everything happened there. The movie houses, the Eden, the Paramount and the Orpheum were there. The Fifth Third and Provident Banks were there. McDevitt's Men's Shop was on the Paramount Building corner and the cigar store on the opposite, southeast corner.

The reason Peebles Corner was so big and wide was because it was the main north-south (Gilbert Avenue) and east-west (McMillan Street) intersection in Walnut Hills. The city eventually built a concrete island with a tall concrete and steel pole between the cigar store and the ice cream store, opposite corners on Gilbert Avenue. That was the widest part of the intersection. The main purpose of the pole was to support the straddling electric lines for street cars (and later trolley buses) running up, down or turning at Peebles Corner.

However, the island also became a safe halfway point when trying to cross the intersection. People seldom made it across Gilbert Avenue on one green light. Unless, of course, you were a paper boy and you ran across Gilbert like we did. Especially when we were peddling our way toward the "King of the Hill" contest, three long city blocks away, down to McMillan and the Parkway.

I don't want to forget the Ice Cream Store, next to the Fifth Third Bank, right on the southwest corner of Peebles Corner. We could buy a tall, cylindrical scoop of ice cream for only a nickel. Can you believe that? And the ice cream had to have stood three to four inches tall on the cone. They called it a Skyscraper and they even put a cherry on top. Now, that was an ice cream cone.

CHAPTER 28

High School Dances – And where do you live?

I WENT TO MY SISTER ANITA'S high school dances because of the other older gals there, of course. Anita was a freshman and I was only interested in seniors and juniors, in that order. However, I had a special rule that my first dance was always with my sister Anita. There were times when this may have upset some young ladies who thought they were going to be my exclusive partner for the evening. This is the way it would happen. I would ask a gal who was a good Jitterbug dancer to, "Save me a Jitterbug." I didn't mean by that request that I was going to be her date that night. No way, that's not the rules of the game my buddies and I played by.

By the way, why do girls expect you to be their one and only after the first kiss or whatever? Are girls programmed before birth and their response is triggered by the kiss? I've often wondered about this. I can see the headlines now: EXTRA! EXTRA!......KISS TRIGGERS CHROMOSOMAL RESPONSE!

At a dance my buddies and I would stand around like everyone else and look over the field of play. We got to know that this group of girls lived in Norwood and that group lived in Silverton and another group came down from Montgomery. Of course, we knew all the gals from our neighborhood and around Peebles Corner, but they were not who we were interested in that night. Why is that, you may ask? Well, for several reasons. First and foremost, we all wanted to get laid. Not that it happened that frequently, if at all, you understand. But we are talking about the basic male hormonal drive in sixteen, seventeen and eighteen year old guys. And we generally didn't fool around with gals from our neighborhood, period. They were more like sisters or cousins to us. That is certainly how I felt. This phenomenon, whether strange or understandable, would stay with me for life.

Another reason we were picky about where the girls lived was transportation. My buddies and I didn't have cars. Hell, neither did our dads. If we went anywhere, it had to be by street car, bus or shoe leather. Some of these gals lived in the boonies.

Ok, here is male logic at work again. Their high schools were usually one hour or more traveling distance from our homes. And places like Montgomery, Silverton or Blue Ash were yet another hour further away. Our best hope would be to discover, and God knows how we searched, for gals who lived between our homes and their schools. Besides, we were always looking for new challenges and, with them, the possibility of new rewards.

And then one night, at her high school dance, my sister introduced me to one of her student friends. My life was about to change drastically, but I had no idea at the time. My sister and I had already danced the first Jitterbug number. My buddies and I were standing out in the school corridor. "Joe, I want you to meet my friend Millie," Anita said. I looked over to the girl standing slightly behind her and my knees almost collapsed on me. She was absolutely gorgeous! She was taller than Anita and bigger in all the right places. Her high cheek bones framed the most beautiful eyes I had ever seen. "Hi," I think I said. I was still kind of stupefied. "Oh," I said, "these are my friends Tony Wass and Tony D'Ang." She asked, "Will you dance the next Jitterbug with me?" I said "Yeah, sure, where will you be standing?" I asked this because there were but a few chairs at school dances in auditoriums. She said, "I'm with friends over by the stage." "I'll be looking for you," she said as she and Anita walked away.

"Holy shit," one Tony said. "You lucky bastard," said the other. I just stood there, still numb from the experience. "Ah Hell," I said, "she may not even be a good Jitterbugger." "Are you nuts?" Wass asked. "Who gives a shit if she Jitterbugs, just find out where she lives." "What do her friends look like?" one of them asked, as we looked through the entrance toward the stage. You see? Male hormonal drive and male logic at work once again. The first question was, "Where do they live?" and the second question was, "What do they look like?" That was our basic approach to all girls in high school and we seldom deviated from it.

CHAPTER 29

Intro to Sex - The Pains of Knowledge

HAVEN'T WE ALL ASKED OURSELVES, "When and how did I first learn about sex?" Well, it wasn't a difficult question for me to answer. I distinctly remember that sex entered my life, rather painfully I might add, at the tender age of six. Momma's friend Ruth was leaving our upstairs flat in the Mayburn Apartments after a visit. They both continued to chat as Ruth started down the first flight of stairs. She said her fourth goodbye to Momma and me as she reached the half-floor landing, when IT happened. And suddenly all hell broke loose.

It appears that I chose that moment in my young life to show off my brand new, grown up salutation that I had learned from the kids in the alley when I said, "Fuck you, Ruth." Just as I saw the shocked expression on Ruth's face, I felt the back of my Momma's hand smack me right in the mouth. Hey, Momma bloodied my lip. So much for my first attempt to enter the world and language of grownups. Of course, they probably laughed about the incident to themselves later, but I never forgot the sting of that lesson in my early education.

Then there was Madeline who played with us smaller kids in the alley behind the Mayburn. She was old enough to have breasts like grownup ladies had. One day somebody found two large and empty cardboard furniture boxes. We built a makeshift box house with two attached rooms and we all climbed in. Madeline said she would show us her breasts, but she wouldn't let us touch them. Let's be honest here, they were her breasts but we kids called them "tits," even Madeline. The next thing I know, we are all showing our hairless pricks and pussys. That's all folks, just a little "You show me yours and I'll show you mine" experience, except this was my first showing.

Once while walking to the drug store to pick something up for Momma, a grown up lady stopped me on McMillan Street and asked me if I would do her a favor for a nickel. I said, "Yes, mam," as I had visions of an ice cream cone from the drug store. "What is it you want done, mam?" I asked.

"Tie my shoe."

"What was that, mam?" I asked.

"Tie my shoe, damnit! You can tie a shoe?"

"Oh, yes, mam," I said as I got down on both my knees and did so.

I was especially careful to make the bow of her shoe strings with two equal length ends. When I was sure the bow was tightly drawn, I looked up at her. At that very moment, she smiled as she lifted up the skirt of her dress over my head. I was looking right up under her skirt, past her stockings and past her knees. Her pure white thighs ended at a dark patch up there. I knew that she saw me staring. She just smiled, put her skirt down and gave me a nickel. She promptly turned and walked away down McMillan, toward Peebles Corner before I could get up off my knees.

I never saw that woman again. And believe me, I looked for her every time I passed that corner by the drug store for the next five years. The mystery of sex thickened for me that day.

Over the years, I never understood why I felt a sense of shame over that little incident. Did I whore for her? Did I really sneak-a-peek or did she purposely slip her skirt up over my head for some kind of thrill? Another of my life's many unanswered questions was added to the list.

Then there was the day a bunch of us kids were playing in the alley behind the Pennington Bakery and it started to rain. We continued playing until it began raining harder, then we all ran to the back of the Boone Street Apartments and hurried down the rear steps into its basement.

Unlike the tall Mayburn Building where I lived, the Boone Street Apartments were two separate, sprawling three story buildings with their entrances fronting on Boone Street. The door we entered led to the boiler room where it was always warm and dry. We guys were pleased that we reached shelter before we were all soaked, but the girls in their thin summer dresses didn't fare as well. They were all so wet that their dresses clung to their skin. And I found myself getting excited about that.

Jo Ann was playing with us that day and she was a couple years older than the rest of us. We were eight and nine years old at the time and Jo Ann was almost eleven. She sometimes tried to act tougher than the rest of us for some reason, but most of the time she would be a lot of fun. We liked Jo Ann a lot, partly because she was older and wiser and therefore, different from the rest of us.

Well, that day, while the rain acted as a curtain to the outside world, Jo Ann proved her difference. We were all sitting on the concrete floor of the boiler room when Jo Ann said, "I'll let you touch my pussy for a nickel." Only a few of us were lucky enough to avail ourselves of her generous offer. My only nickel made it possible for me to have one less mystery in my young life. I wonder what the years and inflation did for Jo Ann and her prices?

CHAPTER 30

Alice - The Early Bird

MOMMA ASKED, "WHY DO YOU have to be at school so early tomorrow?" And I replied, "Because we're having mid-term exams and I want to get there early and review my material so it is fresh in my mind for the test." She bought it! So each day, for a week, Momma woke me up two hours earlier than usual for high school mid-term exams. What Momma didn't know was that I had a prearranged date with Alice every morning that week at her house and in her bed before I went to school.

It went like this. I would take the street car to Evanston Avenue and get off by the Hoffman Public Grade School ballfield. Around 6:45 A.M. Alice's mom and dad would leave their apartment building. He would catch the next street car going toward Norwood and she would take the first street car going toward Peebles Corner. When both were well on their way, I would cross the street and go into Alice's apartment building.

I would climb the stairs to the second floor apartment and knock gently on the door. Alice would open the door sleepily, kiss me hello and retreat quickly back into her bedroom. I forgot to mention that this was early January and it was damn cold outside. Her apartment was a warm haven to me after waiting outside for twenty minutes for her parents to leave. I would quickly undress and climb into Alice's warm bed with her.

I ignored the early morning taste of her kisses because the rest of our love making made up for it. I was seventeen and didn't want to quit, but she had to get up and get ready to go to school herself, so we would restrict our passion to as much as we could squeeze into forty-five minutes. Only once was I successfully able to plead for her to be a half hour late for school. This went on for five straight days.

Oh, and I passed all my exams also. Is there a case here for physical exertion prior to mental challenges? Maybe, but I know for sure that those were the most memorable mid-term exams I ever had. To my good teachers in high school and teachers everywhere, your forgiveness please. I have sought prayerful forgiveness for these and all of my life's indiscretions. However, youth must be served as they say. Now, I can only vaguely remember why. But that's life.

CHAPTER 31

Father Leonard - Our Pastor

FATHER LEONARD DID A LOT for us kids and our relatively poor parish. More than anything else, he pulled his parishioners together. The highlight of his success, to me, was the Mt. Carmel Minstrels. Our small parish had always been known for putting on plays. My mother even took part in some when she was a young lady and the dialogue was all in Italian. The various Sodalities or Holy Name organizations would organize a play or music festival occasionally.

But when Father Leonard came to Mt. Carmel and with the help of key parishioners, like Larry Lavatore and others, a bigger challenge was attempted. They decided to produce a full fledged Al Jolson and Eddy Cantor type Minstrel Show. Can you believe that? A small Italian Church putting on a Minstrel Show with music, singing, dancing and joke telling? Sounds crazy, doesn't it? But guess what? The Mt. Carmel Minstrels proved to be the church's most successful enterprise ever. The Minstrels were usually financially successful, but more importantly, they were very rewarding to the participants and their families.

Where did the talent come from? The parishioners provided most of the talent. The Church Choir provided the bulk of the singers for the Minstrel Chorus and several End Man positions. Rosella, Tina, Ree Ree, Tootsie, they were all in it. Bob and I were End Men. The End Men had the responsibility of telling jokes and singing or dancing solos. Now Bob Dixon and I were somewhat trained singers, but the other End Men were just ushers in the church and the like. When the others did their solos, it was comedic, and the audience of friends and family would howl with laughter; but when Bob and I did ours, it was serious stuff. And damn good I might add.

The Holy Name Sodalities volunteered to underwrite the materials for costumes and staging. Out of five of the funniest and talented Sunday Offering Collectors, four became End Men and Larry Lavatore was the handsome and dashing Mr. Interlocotor. A variety of acts were performed by other parishioners or their children, like tap dancing by Weesee Andrews, Al Jolson impersonations by one of the children, and solos by members of the chorus, like Beta Steven's great swoon song.

However, the biggest treat of all was Father Leonard's friend from Detroit who was invited and accepted to join us. His name was Dick Contino. He was a superstar and already a legend with the accordion. Do you remember his rendition of "Lady of Spain?" Well, Mr. Contino made that recording an international hit. And here he was at our little church in Little Italy to perform with us. Wow, what a thrill!

I can remember all of us rehearsing in the basement of the church, knowing that Dick Contino was to join us after having dinner with Father Leonard. We were buzzing with excitement, and everyone was trying to second guess what number will he play for us later that night. Most of us expected him to play his big hit, "Lady of Spain."

When they finally entered the rehearsal hall, we all stopped what we were doing to see what this international star looked like in person. The girls started "Ooohing and aaahing," and we guys were very excited, too. Father introduced Dick to us all and after a few nods and handshakes, the young and handsome Dick Contino reached for his accordion case. He grabbed a tall stool, put his accordion straps over his shoulders and sat down. The room went dead quiet.

Folks, Dick Contino played the most beautiful rendition of "Ave Maria" that I have ever heard. We were all surprised but also very pleased with his selection. After all, this was the basement of our church and Dick Contino was honoring Our Lady Of Mt. Carmel in the best way he knew how. What a grand moment in time. I will never forget it.

CHAPTER 32

Cassanova - The Minstrel

THE MT. CARMEL MINSTRELS GREW to be one of the best known church shows in town. The first minstrel was produced in 1945 and they became an annual event for the next four years. The first two minstrels were held in the basement of the Mt. Carmel Church. But because they were so popular and seating in the basement hall was so limited, the third production of the minstrels was moved to the University of Cincinnati's Wilson Auditorium.

I don't believe our church made a lot of money on this production because of the expense of the auditorium. However, attendance continued to be greater than ever before. The fourth and final Mt. Carmel Minstrel Show was staged at the famous Taft Auditorium in downtown Cincinnati.

The Church Choir, Bob, Rosella, Tina, Ree Ree, myself and the rest made up the nucleus of the cast and chorus. But we youngsters were surprised to see how much talent the older folks in the Church had. We didn't realize that these older people in our church had performed many times over the years in parish shows and plays. Other neighborhood kids filled in to give us a large Minstrel Chorus and other specialty acts.

A minstrel show usually consisted of a two or three tiered chorus of brightly colored costumed singers. Traditionally, they would each have tambourines to shake after an End Man tells a joke, and certainly laugh and howl with each telling. Picture a high school auditorium bleacher and that is how the chorus is seated behind the main players, the End Men: two, three or four seated stage left and the same number seated stage right. In front of the chorus, center stage, sat Mr. Interlocotor in white tuxedo or tails.   Mr. Interlocotor is like a master of ceremonies who questions the various End Men, basically setting up topics and jokes. The joke telling was between End Men, for example:

> Casanova (me): "Rastus, who was that woman I saw you with last night?"
>
> Rastus (Bob): "That was no woman, that was my wife!"

And on and on it went for about two hours of jokes, dances, novelty acts and songs. Mr. Interlocotor would make all the introductions for the ensemble. The End Men were dressed in a variety of costumes fitting the nature of the characters they were playing. Zoot Suits for Bob and myself, farmer's bib overalls for another, a train conductor's uniform for another, and so on. And yes, the End Men were in black face makeup, even Bob. The Minstrel Show had its beginnings on Show Boats playing the Mississippi, Missouri and Ohio Rivers. Cincinnati was a typical stop on a Show Boat's tour in the late 1800's.

CHAPTER 33

Kenton Street

THE OLD, SINGLE STORY FRAME house we lived in on Kenton Street is gone now. Only an empty parking lot remains of what was our home. Mom would say, "Our house was as busy as Grand Central Station." Of course, my buddies and I hung out there and my sister and her girlfriends were usually around somewhere. They would go into Mom and Pop's bedroom and try to listen in to our bull sessions outside on the front porch but we usually knew they were there.

The one thing that Mom could always count on was that we were all hungry. "Mom, when do we eat?" And in the next breath, "Mom, can Tony (or Millie or Cheri) stay and eat with us?" I can't remember Mom ever refusing anyone an opportunity to sit at our table. And could she cook! Not just the pastas, like our favorite, mostaccioli, but beef stew, pork roast and sauerkraut, liver and onions (even though she personally hated it), beef stroganoff, Hungarian goulash, ham and cabbage, hamburgers and on and on the variety goes. My own extra special favorite, usually on my birthday, was homemade cavatelli. The aromas in our house would start anyone salivating. So naturally my buddies weren't immune to its spells or smells.

Tony Wass was a frequent diner with us and Cheri Dep became aware of that real fast. Consequently, it wasn't long before Tony and Cheri both were joining us for dinner. Before long Tony and Cheri became real friendly. Gee, aren't we surprised? Not to be outdone by those two, Millie and Tony D'Ang started seeing each other too. I can't say that either couple dated at that stage, but they walked each other home. Inevitably, the dating did happen.

I believe Tony Wass and Cheri hung around together for a month or so, but Millie and Tony D'Ang are still together to this day! Were they a match made in Heaven? Possibly, but I like to think of their romance as a match made at Momma Stella's table in our little house on Kenton Street, Little Italy, U.S.A. Neither Frank, Joe Al or I became too friendly with the girls in our neighborhood. I think that was because our intentions were not really that honorable, as you will discover. It wasn't too long before Tony Wass saw the light, said farewell to Cheri and joined the rest of us in our relentless pursuit of? Sex of course. This overwhelming new passion would take us all to the strangest of places. We found ourselves away from Little Italy in unfamiliar neighborhoods doing a variety of different social activities. But we were always aware that first and foremost our goal was sex and meeting the girls who would provide it. Our challenge, of course, was that we had to work our way through a lot of girls who could provide sex to get to those that would provide sex. And what a grand time it was for all of us new men.

CHAPTER 34

The Front Porch

AFTER LEAVING ENGLISH WOODS, and my own bedroom, for a smaller frame house on Kenton Street, we found we had too much furniture.

Consequently, the California style heavy redwood living room sofa and chair, with its wild and bright floral design and padded cushions, ended up on the front porch. The arm rests were wide and flat and large enough for someone to sit on. I loved that furniture and I saw to it that my buddies and I spent a lot of time on the front porch. In retrospect, how tacky looking the front porch must have been? However, Mom and Pop weren't about to throw out good furniture just because they didn't have a living room anymore as we had in English Woods.

From the front porch the boys and I could watch the passing parade of people, especially girls, going up and down Kenton Street. And just about everyone used Kenton and May to get to McMillan Street, the streetcar line or to Peebles Corner, where we thought the real action was. Eventually we wised up to the fact that my sister Anita and her friends were listening in on us and we moved our headquarters to the corner of Kenton and Wayne streets, a couple of houses up Kenton from Joey A's house. There were steps we could sit on while we talked, sang, told jokes, shared experiences with girls (none!) with each other.

So what did my sister and her girl friends do? Why, they moved their listening post over to Millie's house on the other side of Wayne Street. Ah yes, the girls were dumb like foxes. But there was an unusual happening on our corner one night that none of us guys would ever forget.

CHAPTER 35

Good Thing

I DOUBT THAT ANY OF US GUYS can remember her name now, but this girl would walk by our corner every now and then coming from Peebles Corner. We'd say "Hello" to her and so forth, but one of my buddies (and you know who you are) asked, "Would you like for me to walk you home?" And she said, "Yes." Well, well, WELL!

I don't remember how long it took for those walks home to become sex under the Burbank Bridge, but once it happened, it was repeated every time she came by Our Corner with one or the other of us. Tony D'Ang was the exception because he was saving himself for someone very special, but we didn't know that at the time. Consequently, Tony got teased by us a lot. "Come on, you cherry, this is your chance," and stuff like that.

We all knew who her favorite was (unnamed here), but she didn't refuse any show of attention from the rest of us. Hence, we gave her the nickname, "Good Thing." She gave our growing up process a real boost. Thanks a million, Good Thing! And everyone please forgive me if my remarks appear sexist, but sometimes the truth, from a different age, appears so. After a while, we figured out that the punks, my sister and friends, could hear us talk on the corner from Millie's listening post. What to do? Why, we just moved farther up Kenton to the corner of McMillan and checked out the many sights that it had to offer.

CHAPTER 36

McMillan Street

YOU KNOW HOW THEY SAY, "Broadway is the Heart of New York?" Well that's how we felt about McMillan Street and its relation to Peebles Corner in Walnut Hills. Our lives were to be guided by the streets into, off of and intersecting with McMillan Street for most of our formative years. At least through high school, McMillan Street was the main artery into the heart of our lives.

For example, the main drug store serving Little Italy was Bogers Drug Store across from the end of Kenton Street on McMillan. The German bakery and butcher shop (remember Grandma Anna?) were also across McMillan Street from Kenton as were other small retail shops.

My cousin Frank, Uncle Sebastian's son, operated a bar, the Old Hickory, on McMillan between May and Kenton Streets. I would end up working there as a bar boy after school. You know, sweep the floors, sort the beer and pop bottles by brand name, wipe off tables and such.

My cousin Frank was afraid the police would notice that I was under age, I was fifteen at the time, so he asked me to grow a mustache. Try as I did, the best I could do was to create some peach fuzz looking thing above my upper lip. The ladies that frequented the bar after working at their various defense plants would tease me about it, but said it indeed made me look older. They were just kidding me, but my buddies quickly picked-up on this, and for longer that I care to remember, nicknamed me "Young Cunt." Yep, growing up can be tough.

CHAPTER 37

The Old Hickory Cafe

MY COUSIN FRANK AND HIS wife at the time, Betty, lived above the Old Hickory Café. Poppa Nick would come up and help out some nights after dinner, usually on Friday nights when the bar was so busy. However, that would piss off my mother and eventually Poppa gave it up.

I enjoyed this new atmosphere personally. I thought it was like some fantasy playground. Little did I realize then that in reality it was a sexual playground for the customers. We all understand now that during World War II a lot of women took over the jobs that the soldiers and sailors left vacant.

One of the largest defense plants in the Cincinnati area was the Wright Plant, where they manufactured aircraft engines. There was The Cincinnati Machine Tool Company, the US Playing Card Company, where they made parachutes for bombs, and many others.

On a payday Friday these women would flock to the bars like my cousin Frank's to spend their money, drink with their friends, have fun and basically relax. I didn't realize initially that even a fifteen year old like me was fair game to these hard working ladies. Oh, but I was to find out very soon.

One particular payday evening, a group of regular female customers were sitting at the bar and hitting the top of the bar in front of them with little wooden sticks with a wooden ball attached to the end, like a mallet. What a racket they would make with those sticks. What it meant to them and my cousin Frank or his wife Betty, the bartenders, was they wanted another drink. But after they got their drinks they kept banging their sticks on the bar, which meant that now they wanted sex. And any male in the bar was a target for their needs. But wait, when there weren't any other males available in the bar, they kept on pounding their sticks.

That meant they wanted the bartender, my cousin Frank. He would laugh at them and go along with their teasing, but when they turned their attention to me, my cousin Frank stepped in and told them that I was off limits. Frank had to protect me from myself, so to speak. Thanks, cousin Frank. I think?

CHAPTER 38

Uncle Albert

GRANDMA ANNA'S YOUNGEST SON and my mother's brother was my Uncle Albert. Uncle Al played a major role in my life. He was only seven years older than I and therefore not yet on Mt. Olympus like all the other aunts and uncles in my life.

Al lived with Grandma and Grandpa in the Mayburn Apartment Building. However, in my memory, he was away a lot. He went to Windsor School and when he graduated, he went to the Printing School on McMillan Street.

When we lived in the Mayburn, I knew that Al was a good baseball player. Al was a catcher and he would allow me to pretend I was a pitcher and throw baseballs to him in the alley. We would usually go across Burbank to the alley behind Pennington's Bakery, where my Grandfather Tony worked, and play catch. Then one day he went away. I didn't understand what they meant when I heard that Uncle Al had gone to the Minors. I just knew that one day we were playing catch and the next day he was gone.

My hero was gone and there was no one to play catch with. I was heartsick.

Then, some time later (a month? a year?), he came back home. Why? I haven't a clue. But I suspect he was cut from the team. And only a short time after that, Al went away again. This time I was told he joined the Three C's, the Civilian Conservation Corps that President Roosevelt created. So my hero was gone again. I guess I realized then that I couldn't count on him being around for my pleasure.

I have to note for the record that at this time in my Uncle Al's life the strongest drink he ever drank was Coca Cola. And his favorite snack was a Hershey Bar. Ok? I'll explain later.

Then one day Uncle Al was back from the Three C's. I was really confused. It was like the old saying, "Now you see him, now you don't." I believe that's when I decided to find someone else to look up to. I didn't realize it at the time, but that person turned out to be my classmate at Windsor Grade School, Bob Dixon.

And just as I was getting used to Uncle Al being home again, guess what happened? Japan bombed Pearl Harbor.

CHAPTER 39

A United States Marine

AFTER THE SURPRISE ATTACK ON Pearl Harbor on Sunday, Uncle Al and his buddies went downtown on Monday and joined the Army, Navy or Marines. It was that simple, that quick, that decisive. And there he was, gone again. However, this time I had a better understanding of why Al and all the other guys were leaving home. I was young but not stupid. My Poppa Nick fought in World War I and I'd heard some of his stories of horror. These guys were going to War.

This time the whole family, Grandma, Grandpa, Momma, Poppa, all my uncles and aunts were scared for Al's going away. I didn't quite understand that. Didn't we know that Al always comes back? There was a gloom about this departure that I had not witnessed before.

Guess what happened next? He came back! In no time it seemed my Uncle Albert (I've got to get formal now and show the correct respect) came home again. Only this time he was handsome in his new, terrific looking, green Marine uniform.

Wow! My hero was now a giant among men, a United States Marine.

And then he was gone. This time, they told me, for "the duration," whatever that was.

CHAPTER 40

Returning Hero

ALBERT IS BACK! HE'S ALIVE and well, kinda. He's been gone this time for over two years. Al fought at Guadalcanal with the Marines First Division and survived everything the Japanese threw at him, but he wasn't that fortunate with Mother Nature.

We first heard that Al was okay when he was sent to a hospital in Australia suffering with malaria. Later, he was shipped home to the United States and transferred to the Navy Hospital at the Brooklyn Navy Yard. Of course, he was given leave to come home to Cincinnati en route.

I thought, "Who is this guy? How thin and gaunt he looks." There were those big bags under his eyes. "Did he just stagger? Is he drunk?" Didn't he only drink Cokes and eat Hershey Bars? "What in the world happened to him?" Well, as we all know now, a hell of a lot happened to him and the rest of the Marines, soldiers and sailors in that pivotal, first offensive battle in the Pacific by the United States of America against Japan.

My Uncle Albert was one of the lucky survivors. However, the days of youth, Cokes and Hershey Bars were gone forever. And unfortunately Tony Wass's brother was killed on the same island. The two buddies managed to see each other before Tony's brother was killed. How many other buddies, brothers, cousins, didn't make it? Of course, none of us knew the terrible times these men had at the time. We know now and we should all honor them for that.

I'm not an expert, but from what I learned about the nightly bombardment they received from Japanese ships after they had landed, the malaria they couldn't escape, the suicide charges the Japanese made at them time and again, well, it's a miracle he survived. And we thank you Lord for that.

CHAPTER 41

Cleaning the Barber Shop

MY BUDDIES AND I WERE handicapped in a way because I had to complete my assigned chores at my Pop's barber shop before I was free to go out and play. I did this after the shop closed, three times a week.

My usual routine was this: after dinner Poppa Nick would give me the key to the barber shop and my buddies and I would walk up McMillan to the Kemper Lane Hotel, where the shop was located. They would sit around on the waiting chairs and read magazines (*Life, Time, Look, Police Gazette*, etc.) while I swept the floor, mopped the floor, cleaned the three sinks and six mirrors. The front window and door I took care of after school once a week without my friends in attendance.

Now there was a Western Union Office, Walnut Hills Branch, next door to Poppa's barber shop. My friend Jimmy, a man in his twenties, was a delivery boy, by bicycle, for them. Over time, Jimmy introduced me to the ladies and men that worked there. The manager was my Poppa's customer. Anyway, one night, while my buddies were waiting for me to clean up the shop,

Jimmy came over and asked me to "Come on over to the office. Barbara wants to show you something." Barbara was a beautiful, young blonde lady in her early twenties and she and Jimmy were the only ones on duty that night. So I went next door with Jimmy. There were no customers there at the time. Jimmy said, "Barbara, tell him what all the guys ask you to do." She smiled and waved me over to her side of the counter where I had never gone before. She was sitting on one of those small swiveling typist chairs in front of a Teletype machine. When I walked over to her, she swiveled her chair around, showing me her gorgeous crossed legs, with her skirt just above her knees.

She said, "All the men point to my legs and say, *Nice paint job, now show me your pretty white skin.*" At which time, she raised her skirt up her thighs, above her painted leg line, showing her white flesh. Well, I was paralyzed. There I was, stunned with the view of this beautiful women's thighs. My knees must have buckled.

Jimmy and Barbara just laughed at me. But regaining my composure I asked, "If I bring my friends over, would you show them that trick?" Barbara said, "Oh sure," enjoying my embarrassment and shyness. Of course, I dashed back to the barber shop and hollered, "Quick, everybody come over to the

Western Union Office. You're going to meet that beautiful blonde lady." They just about knocked me over getting out of Poppa's shop. Again, Barbara told her little ditty to my friends. Oh my God! We had never seen anything so beautiful and titillating in our young lives. You can guess the status of our composure at the time.

For Barbara, it was probably a humorous version of the Dance of the Seven Veils. For us, it was a view of Paradise. Then Jimmy said, "OK fellas, that's it. We've got to get back to work now."

We all gushed out our thanks to Barbara and Jimmy and returned to the barber shop. I believe it took us a little time to recover from the show. Let me say right here that there never was another demonstration like that ever again. And I believe I can speak for my friends when I say that after that adventure we hoped for something exciting like this to happen to us every time we went to my Pop's shop at night, but to no avail.

Sometimes it was tough to be a teenager, real tough. But the memory? Well, that folks is wonderful. Oh yeah.

CHAPTER 42

The Great Flood of 1937

MY GRANDMA ANNA LIVED FOR 92 years. Widowed at least three times, she bore sixteen children. However, only four of her children survived to adulthood. The oldest of the four was my Uncle John, then Aunt Mary, my momma Stella and the youngest was Uncle Albert.

When the terrible flood of 1937 hit Cincinnati, one of the first problems it created for Little Italy, protected from the Ohio River way up on Walnut Hills, was the shortage of fresh water. I don't know the technical reasons why a shortage existed, but I certainly remember one of the solutions. We found a fresh water spring.

At that time there were two tunnels over the railroad tracks that ran through Little Italy, a short tunnel that ran under McMillan Street and a much longer tunnel about a quarter of a mile farther up the line. Luckily, there was a fresh water spring inside the long tunnel that spilled out of its side wall.

Everyday long lines of people would take buckets and other containers to this spring to capture fresh water for their families. I was only eight years old at the time, but I remember an adult taking me along to fetch water. We would bypass the steps under the Burbank Street Bridge because Merkle Brothers Pipe and Ditto Press located under the bridge were impassable to us. We would walk up Boone Street and access the railroad track just south of McMillan Street. Walking through the first and shortest of the two tunnels was a scary experience for me. When we got to the long tunnel, people were waiting in a long line extending from the tunnel's entrance.

People waited their turn in an orderly manner. I remember neighbors and friends chatting while we all stood in line. We kids took advantage of this time to have fun playing with each other. I don't remember how long we had to repeat this routine, but I do remember how difficult it was for everyone to carry the water back to their homes. It was about a mile back to the Mayburn Apartments for me.

One day there was a big commotion in front of Grandma Anna's apartment on Burbank Hill, where a large city tanker truck was parked. Soon Grandma Anna and my Uncle Johnny came out of her apartment with an empty water tub. He had driven the truck to our neighborhood. Uncle Johnny put the tub under a spigot on the truck and filled it with fresh water. To us, after many trips to the long tunnel, it was a miracle.

People poured out of their apartments and houses and lined up at the truck for a portion of fresh water, thanks to my Uncle Johnny. However, he wasn't able to stay long because he had other locations in the city to take his fresh water to. I remember there was a bit of a frenzy and some name calling when Uncle Johnny had to close his spigot and leave. Not everyone was happy with that decision, but I'll always remember that my Uncle Johnny was a hero to all that got fresh water that day in 1937. Of course, he had always been a hero to me.

CHAPTER 43

Coney Island and the Island Queen

HOW MANY PEOPLE HAD THE opportunity of taking a boat ride on the famous steam powered paddle boat, the Island Queen, to an amusement park named Coney Island on the shore of the Ohio River? Only those of us lucky enough to live in Cincinnati, Ohio, in the 30's and 40's. They were the special family outings when I was a child, the magic of the Island Queen with the power of its steam driven arms giving life to its rear paddle wheels. There was the constant vibration to the boat as she churned her way upriver to Coney Island. Then there was the mystery of her several decks, just like a woman, don't you think? Of course when I got older the upper deck would have a special purpose for me. Privacy, to share with a special someone. Yes, I have fond memories of the Island Queen's upper deck.

After the boat docked at Coney Island, my family would walk the path to picnic area and claim a table, or more, for ourselves. Baskets of food were placed on the table and covered with a table cloth to protect it from insects and announce our ownership. Then we would go into the amusement park proper and have our fun. Sometimes someone would stay back with the table and protect the food, or if we recognized a friend at another table, they sometimes volunteered to watch the table for us. People were helpful to one another in that way.

Everyone had their favorite ride at Coney Island. Mine was the Airplane Ride, where you could make your plane go left or right by pushing the big front rudder left or right. I was bedazzled by the experience. Of course, it really was just a big swing that went around in ever increasing circles, attached to a center post. We children chose to ignore that fact and let our imaginations run wild. I shot down many an enemy Fokker airplane on that ride.

Momma didn't ride, she just watched us while eating her favorite treat, Coney Island's famous soft ice cream cones. Poppa Nick would take my sister Anita on the merry-go-round and rides like that. There was a small roller coaster that we enjoyed, too. When it was time to go back to the picnic table and eat, we would say, "Oh Poppa, just one more ride. Please?" Like parents everywhere, sometimes they relented and sometimes they didn't. Eventually, however, we all gathered back at our table of goodies.

Today, everyone is aware of the need for refrigeration, coolers and the like, to prevent food spoilage. But back then we didn't have a clue. For a typical meal Momma Stella would have fried chicken, lasagna, meatballs, salad, greens, bread and butter. And if we were with others, like Aunt Mary and Uncle Julius, there might be watermelon for dessert. Yes, folks, it was wonderful, just wonderful and guess what? I don't remember anyone getting sick from food poisoning either.

Of course, the menus varied with each outing, but my God, what a way to spend a summer's day in Cincinnati, Ohio. I don't for a minute mean to imply that we went to Coney Island every Sunday because we didn't. Neither my family or any other family we knew could afford to do that. We were in the middle of the Great Depression and if we got to Coney Island once, twice or even three times a summer, we felt very lucky.

After our picnic, we kids would beg our parents again for "just one more ride" or at least a walk through the amusement area. The key to our parents answer was how long before the Island Queen arrived from its next trip upriver for our return boat ride to the city. If we had time, this is when I preferred to go to the Carnival area, where I got to shoot a real rifle with bullets at targets, even moving ones. Whereas, my sister Anita liked to fish and Poppa Nick saw to it that we each satisfied our desires.

I thought it strange that Poppa Nick, after being in the Big War, didn't care to shoot the target rifles like I did. I didn't know then that Poppa Nick swore to himself never to shoot a rifle again as long as he lived.

When we heard the Island Queen's whistle blow, we all went back to the picnic area and gathered up our stuff and walked down to the boat landing. I was always fascinated with how the Island Queen's captain directed his boat into the Coney Island dock. He actually had to go up river a bit before he could turn the boat around and slowly make his way back down river and into the dock on the Ohio shore. It was great fun to watch this majestic boat come to the landing, the sailors aboard throw their ropes to the men on shore to pull the boat to its resting position and then securely tie it down. Then the men on board would lower the long walkway or plank to the shore so their current passengers could go ashore and when emptied, the captain blew the whistle for boarding.

Everyone returning to the city waited in line until the whistle for boarding blew. Again, we boarded the boat for our return trip down river. When all were aboard and the plank raised from the shore, the captain would blow the whistle again, announcing our backing off from shore and heading back to the city.

The return home was always a little fuzzy for me. We kids had worn ourselves out at the park and had eaten a big meal. Now the steady swoosh, swoosh, swoosh of the boat's steam engine's piston arms and the ever present vibration that the engine created would rock Anita and me to sleep. We would be awakened to someone saying, "Wake up, we're home."

Poppa would end up carrying Anita, still asleep, up the Broadway Street Landing, while Momma and I would carry our picnic baskets and any prizes we may have won at Coney Island. Finally, our streetcar would arrive and bring us up Gilbert Avenue to Kenton Street, its bridge, Little Italy and home.

Yes folks, I do miss it so.

CHAPTER 44

Aunt Mary and Uncle Julius

WHEN WE LIVED IN THE Mayburn Apartment Building, there would be a frequent visitor, my Aunt Mary. She and Uncle Julius lived on Kenton Street, south of Burbank, leading toward the Kenton Street Bridge and Gilbert Avenue. Momma Stella and Aunt Mary have been buddies, besides being sisters, since their hardship days growing up in Lynch Mines, Kentucky.

Sometimes, when I was outside playing, Momma would open her kitchen window and call out to me from the fifth floor apartment. "Jo Jo, I need you to go to the store for me," she would say. When Aunt Mary was there that usually meant that I would be buying five loose Chesterfield cigarettes for Momma and five Lucky Strikes for Aunt Mary. Heinemen Groceries sold loose cigarettes during the War when they were so difficult to get. Heinemen's was located one block north on May Street and on the corner with Morgan.

Oh, there would be other things to buy for Momma like bread, milk, etc., but trust me, the main reason for my trip was cigarettes for the ladies. Sometimes other lady friends would join them and my order would be expanded to Camels and other brands. These friends usually included Adeline Brockman, a beautiful redhead and the lovely Bellchore sisters.

I don't know if Poppa Nick and Uncle Julius knew Momma and Aunt Mary smoked cigarettes at that time. Money being tight for everyone in those days makes me doubt it. I believe they cost a penny a piece during the War, and we didn't have too many loose pennies hanging around.

After dinner in their respective homes, Poppa Nick and Uncle Julius would take long walks together. Of course that meant Momma and Aunt Mary would get together, too. That was before Aunt Mary got pregnant with my cousin Tommy and Momma with my twin sisters Marie and Margurite. After that, their loose cigarette days were over.

Uncle Julius loved my little sister Anita. She was definitely his favorite. He also knew that I was fascinated with his working at Davis Tailoring, located on the south side and below Goose Neck Hill. Many of the people in Little Italy worked there. That's where Uncle Julius met Larry Lavatore, and soon they started a tailoring business on the side in Larry's attic.

I loved looking through his men's style books from Milan, Italy. He would say, "That's the style of suit that Clark Gable wears." Over the years Uncle Julius made me a variety of clothes, but the highlight was when my sister Anita got married and he made blue serge suits for all the men in the wedding, including the groom. Let me tell you folks, we men looked real sharp and my sister Anita has the wedding pictures to prove it. The art of tailoring has somewhat disappeared today. We don't seem to have time for fittings and things like that. Today we seem to settle for mediocrity because we are all in such a hurry.

God, how I wish I could have joined Poppa Nick and Uncle Julius in one of their long walks together. What did they talk about? What could I add that would be of interest to two men born in Italy, a tailor and a barber, and me. Now that I think about it, I couldn't have added much of interest. They already knew everything worth knowing, living in *LITTLE ITALY: May, Burbank and Boone.*

AUTHOR'S FINAL NOTE

I SPENT OVER TEN YEARS writing and rewriting *LITTLE ITALY: May, Burbank and Boone*. For me, it was a labor of love. I wanted to acknowledge all the families that lived in Little Italy during the years I covered in this text, but I found that to be impossible.

Several lists of family names were drawn up, only for me to discover later that some names had been forgotten. I refuse to slight any of those wonderful families by neglecting to include them on such a list. Therefore, no list, just *Remembrances*.

You all know who you are and where we all came from. I only have one thing to ask you. Was *Little Italy* as wonderful for you as it was for me?

Joe Martinelli

Printed in the United States
24014LVS00006BA/104